THE BOOK of CHRISTMAS

The Book of
CHRISTMAS

Marguerite Ickis

With drawings by Miriam F. Fabbri and J. V. Miller

Christmas in Europe illustrated by Dr. Miklos Foghtuy

DODD, MEAD & COMPANY   NEW YORK

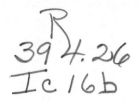
TO LOUISE

who loved Christmas

CONTENTS

THE BOOK of CHRISTMAS

CHRISTMAS IS COMING, HURRAH!

1. HOW MANY DAYS OF CHRISTMAS?

"How many days of Christmas?" is a question which might be answered in various ways, like that of the nursery pilgrims, "How far is it to Babylon?" It all depends on your position and whether Old World customs are still observed in the home or community. Christmas of old was a much longer season, with many special days both before and after December 25, but here in America it mostly begins on Christmas Eve and ends with a New Year's celebration. However, many people, even those who do not observe it in any way, have a certain wistful sentiment for Twelfth-night, and often keep their Christmas trees in order to enjoy their beauty and fragrance a few extra days.

Candlemas, the feast of the Purification of the Virgin on February 2, and Christmas are linked in an old Scottish weather forecast, more romantic than the one we are familiar with:

> "If Candlemas Day be bright and fair,
> The half of winter is to come and mair:
> If Candlemas be wet and foul,
> The half of winter's gone at Yule."

Children love to follow the tradition of forecasting weather for the coming year. It is said that whatever the weather on each day of the Twelve Days of Christmas, so will be each of the succeeding months in the coming year.

In this book you will find Christmas lore and suggestions for holiday celebrations in churches, schools, clubs, and community centers. One whole section is devoted to family activities. With the workday world demanding constant attention to practical affairs, the long Christmastide of forty days is out of the question for most of us, but twelve days out of the year are few enough for the feast of peace and good will and merrymaking, so, if at all possible, plan to have at least "Twelve Days of Christmas."

1

2. CHRISTMAS GREETINGS

From a Fairy to a Child

Lady, dear, if Fairies may
    For a moment lay aside
Cunning tricks and elfish play,
    'Tis at happy Christmastide.

We have heard the children say —
    Gentle children, whom we love —
Long ago, on Christmas Day,
    Came a message from above.

Still, as Christmastide comes round,
    They remember it again —
Echo still the joyful sound
    "Peace on earth, good will to men!"

Yet the hearts must childlike be
    Where such heavenly guests abide;
Unto children, in their glee,
    All the year is Christmastide.

Thus forgetting tricks and play
    For a moment, Lady dear,
We would wish you, if we may
    Merry Christmas, glad New Year!

Christmas, 1867   LEWIS CARROLL

3. CHRISTMAS GREENS

Decorating homes and churches with greens is a universal Christmas custom, and people are always seeking new ideas for hanging and arranging them. Our choice of holly, mistletoe and fir derives from many stories and legends. More recently plants with thick waxy leaves — such as laurel, rhododendron, and boxwood — have been added. Perhaps people would use other native flowers and shrubs if they knew how to dry them and add color afterward. Every plant requires some individual attention, but here are a few basic rules that apply to all of them:

1. Flowers or foliage should be picked at peak of maturity, so the harvesting is a continuous process.

2. Flowers that grow in masses or clusters are tied in small bunches and hung upside down to dry. If flowers have flat heads, such as daisies, they can be buried in a box of sand and allowed to remain several weeks until dry.

3. To dry foliage such as autumn leaves or laurel branches, immerse the stems in a solution of one-third glycerin and two parts water. Allow them to remain several weeks or until the water is completely evaporated.

4. Color can be added in many ways. The most convenient is to use a can of opaque paint to which a spraying device is already attached. Sometimes waxy surfaces of leaves or pine cones resist paint; if so, remove the wax with alcohol.

3

CHRISTMAS WREATHS

Christmas Wreaths

Families living near places where evergreens grow can have the pleasure of gathering their own Christmas greens. From pine branches and cones can be made a handsome wreath for the front door, and it can be personalized in any number of ways.

A wreath is made by attaching short pieces of pine to a wire foundation with thin wire or soft string such as jute. If string is used, it should be either green or brown so it can easily be hidden by the branches. The evergreens used in a wreath should be cut into sprays about six inches long; the choice tips of the branches will give it a fuller and denser foliage. At the beginning it is necessary to decide whether all the evergreens will be tied in one direction or whether they will be arranged so they face the top and bottom of the wreath. Select a few sprays in your left hand and tie them to the foundation securely with your right hand. Be sure to wrap the string around all the branches and then around the foundation. A wreath is more attractive when the opening in the center is large; as you go along, you add a little less material to the inside of the wreath than to the outside. You must watch the progress of the outline of the wreath as it is being tied but minor irregularities may be removed with a pair of shears after it is finished.

If you wish to make a more formal wreath and one not quite so large, use boxwood for the greens, or if that is not available, select holly or arborvitae. The Italians substitute bright-colored fruit for red berries, and a boxwood foundation is particularly appropriate for this arrangement because the stiff, shiny leaves have the same texture as the rinds of the fruit.

On the opposite page you will find some novel wreaths which may be new to you. The first (A) requires a wire frame which may be purchased at a florist's shop and which can be used in a number of ways. You may fit the sprays in the wire loops as intended or cover the frame with gold paint and tie on occasional bunches of

5

seed pods, as shown in the picture. The second wreath (*B*) has assorted nuts arranged in a circle and tied into a green wreath. Each nut is wrapped separately in cellophane, which makes them glisten in the light and also aids in fastening them on to the pine. Wreath *C* suggests round flat pieces of green or red peppermint candies, for added color. These are also wrapped in cellophane. The fourth wreath (*D*) is made of plumes — just to be different.

Make a Wreath for the Birds which can be placed outside the window or near the house. Remember, birds are divided into three groups — as far as their diet is concerned — vegetarians (seeds and grasses), meat-eaters, and ones that desire a balanced ration. Birds that stay the winter usually belong to the last two groups, so tie on bits of suet and berries. A good plan is to dip pine cones in melted suet and then roll them in cracked grain or bird seed. Tie the pine cones at intervals around the wreath.

Hanging the Mistletoe is a custom everyone enjoys at a Christmas party because anyone who passes under it may be kissed. One tradition has it "that a lad must remove a berry each time he kisses a maid beneath the mistletoe bough."

It was Queen Elizabeth who said that mistletoe should always be hung in a hall. A novel way to do this is to arrange a pair of embroidery hoops so that the inner one forms another circle crosswise, as shown in the drawing. Wrap each hoop with gold or silver paper, then tie a large clump of mistletoe in the center. Streamers of red and green satin ribbon will add to the gaiety of the decoration.

Another method of making a mistletoe ball is by sticking the stems into a round potato. The moisture will keep the branches fresh, and it will look like a hanging basket. Make holes in the potato with a nail or another sharp instrument in order to insert the stems.

A *Novel Centerpiece* for a mantle or center table decoration can be made by inserting small evergreen sprays into a loaf of bread in such a way that it is completely covered. Decide the size and shape you wish to make. Then try to find a loaf to fit the specification. The moisture in the bread will keep the greens fresh all during the holiday season. It is possible to ornament the arrangement by pushing candles down into the top of the bread, and small Christmas balls and bells can be tied to the sides.

Holly Ball and Tree. If you are not working with fresh holly branches, soak them in water in order to shape them. The tree is made by fastening a metal flower holder on top of a dowel stick to hold the stems.

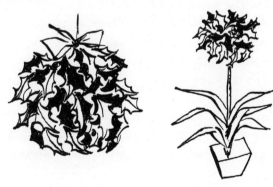

Christmas Tree from Mexico

The inspiration for this elegant tree came after purchasing two dozen white doves, which are sold in many Mexican shops. The body of the bird is a white eggshell; a head is attached to the pointed end of the egg and paper tails and wings, to the sides and rear. The head is carved from a piece of paraffin, then melted slightly at the neckline in order to attach it to the body. The tail and wings consist of fluted white paper which is glued onto the body, and wire feet are added.

The tree was covered with a white plastic spray, and the birds evenly distributed in natural poses. To add some color, the eyes and feet were painted red and small spots of gold were painted on the wings and tail. Garlands of pearls were strung among the branches.

Espalier Christmas Tree

An espalier Christmas tree can be used in many different settings and may be just what you are looking for if you live in a small apartment. The frame, or foundation, is made from heavy wire which can lead out into as many branches as you desire. Attach the wire to the wall with small staples after the greens have been tied in place. You can make the branches entirely of greens or artificial flowers, or you may use both.

This type of tree makes an excellent outdoor decoration, particularly if placed in front of a brick wall or house.

If You Haven't Space for a Tree

Make a tree that can be set against the wall using a ladder-like frame with one-inch dowels inserted in two upright sides and placed eight to ten inches apart. Indicate the tree by twisting green satin ribbon around the rungs in shape of outer edge, as shown in drawing. Hang tree ornaments on inside areas and tie Christmas presents on outer part of rungs or dowels.

Or

Cut a large tree frame out of green cardboard and tack it on to the front of a bookshelf. The tree can be decorated with painted ornaments, snowflakes, or children's toys. To make it look more like a tree, hang real ornaments at the bottom of the shelves; loops of tinsel or popcorn might also be added.

4. ROOM DECORATIONS

Decorate the Walls

Cut strips of red and green paper and fold them in the same kindergarten way, as shown in the sketch. On the top draw a pine tree, balls, Santa Claus, or anything that pleases your Christmas fancy. Cut around the drawing except at one place on each side, which will hold the units together. Use the strips as a frieze to decorate the dining room or nursery.

The children might like to make a Christmas mural for their rooms. Get a large piece of brown wrapping paper and let all take a hand in creating a Christmas scene. You can make your picture with poster paints or construction paper or both. A good way is to spread the paper on the floor and paint in a background before you hang it up — a snow scene or a fireplace, let us say. Then thumbtack it to the wall and use the colored construction paper to put in the figures, houses, trees, etc. Make the figures with a third dimensional effect, if you like. An improvised mural makes a good background for a Christmas tree.

11

MEXICAN ICON AND TRIPTYCH

Tin is a very useful medium for making Christmas decorations, particularly if a party is being given in a large room where a large number of decorations is desirable. Many tin cans have a "gold" lining, so consider whether you want a gold or silver- Christmas and use one color throughout. The Mexicans make very beautiful Christmas and religious ornaments, which are kept from year to year; if you are near a Mexican shop, you will see the candlesticks, crèches, triptychs, and tiny birds used for trimming the tree. They are usually decorated with stamped-in designs, and many are painted in vivid colors — bright pink, gold, or blue — so typical in Mexico.

These gay Christmas tree ornaments can also be made from tin, simply by cutting and bending. To make the star three-dimensional, bend it slightly along the dark middle line running from the apex of the triangles to the middle of the star.

The Christmas tree is made by cutting along the seam of a partially opened tin can and then cutting the walls away from the base, with the exception of one inch, which is left for the trunk of the tree. Cut the walls into half-inch strips and twist them to make the branches more realistic. The star is cut from the lid of the can, which remains attached at the top.

Decorate the Table

Since most current magazines feature novel table decorations in their November and December issues, we are passing them by with only a few comments. One suggestion we would like to make is a tablecloth made of white organdy, to be used throughout the holiday season. Small motifs, such as bells, sprays of holly, or mistletoe can be cut from colored material and appliquéd on to the cloth — either on top or underneath. Even a white snowman can be silhouetted against the transparent organdy.

Here are two types of angels that can easily be made for place settings or for the center of the table.

This little angel is made by wiring a wooden head to the top of a pine cone and extending the wire above so that it can be twisted into a halo. Make the wings of gold paper and paint the tips of the cone to match.

A cone-shaped drinking cup is used for the body of the angel and it has a wooden head. Make ruffles of lace or white crepe paper and use gold and black paint for adding features.

Topiary Trees and Ornaments

These trees and decorations resemble topiary work one finds in a formal garden. They are made by first constructing a foundation of wire netting in the size and shape you desire and fastening it on to a wooden base or stem which can be anchored in a bucket of sand. The wire should be completely covered by sewing on small Christmas tree balls or foliage. This type of decoration is excellent for adding color to doorways or halls.

The candle sconce shown at the top of the illustration is made from tin and ornamented with green and red metallic paper.

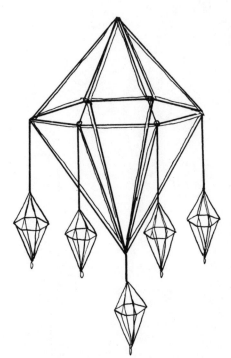

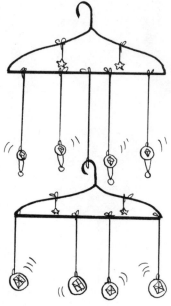

POSTER WITH BELLS

There is no limit to the number of units in a mobile or the variety in their arrangement, as long as they balance in weight and design. The motifs are cut from decorated cardboard or clear plastic and suspended on strands of fine thread.

16

Children love to paint Nativity scenes and Christmas designs on windows; this used to create a problem for Mother, who had to remove them after the holidays were over. Chemists have now developed several transparent paints suitable for use on glass. Dri-Mark, which can be purchased at any handicraft supply house, can be washed off at any time. Another advantage to this paint is that it comes in a tube equipped with a ball point at one end, so no paint brush is required for its application. Dek-All can also be used on glass, but it is permanent and cannot be removed. Artists use it for decorating mirrors, glass screens, coffee-table tops, etc.

Here is an idea for decorating any exposed light bulbs. Use Dri-Mark paint unless you want to make a conventional design that can be enjoyed after the Christmas Season.

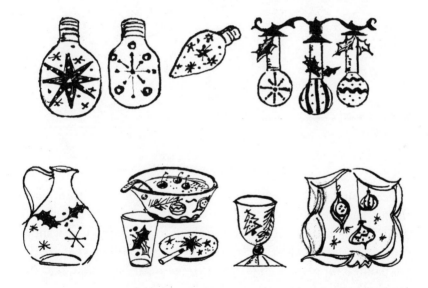

It is great fun to decorate mirrors, ash trays, or windows once you get into the spirit of it. If you are giving a party, add some gay designs to the glasses and punch bowl — the paint is not harmful and can be removed later.

Transparencies

Transparencies can be made either on glass or thin plastic sheets, such as celluloid. If you want them to last, it is best to make them on celluloid and paste them to the window during the Christmas season, then pack them away for another year. If they are painted on glass, some type of frame must be added, and they are also hard to hang.

Either Dek-All or Dri-Mark paint can be used. The Dri-Mark Co. includes a tube of silver paint which can be used for outlining inclusions for receiving the bright colors commonly used in a transparency.

5. CHRISTMAS TREE DECORATIONS

Of course it is possible to buy Christmas ornaments of all descriptions, but it is more fun to make them as part of the Christmas preparation. This is particularly true when there are children in the family.

The simplest way to make a round ball is to cover a round object such as a rubber ball or an orange with papier-mâché. This is done by tearing paper into small pieces, dipping them into starch, and covering the object which has been coated with a thin layer of vaseline. Add two or three layers of the prepared paper pieces, allow them to dry, then cut the sphere in two to remove the mold. Paste the paper halves together again by covering the seam with another layer of paper. It is a good idea to use paper toweling for the final layer to make a suitable background for painting on designs. Very small children can simply paste Christmas seals on to a white surface.

Cornucopias

It would not be a real Christmas tree without cornucopias. There should be a cone-shaped container filled with candy and nuts for every child and guest. Authentic cornucopias were once made of heavy gold paper, decorated with angels. Red and green glossy paper will give equal satisfaction. Sew a row of white popcorn around the top, or trim them in some other way, according to your fancy.

Elegant Tree Balls

These balls are made of papier-mâché, painted gold or silver, with strips of green or red velvet glued onto the background. Seal over the edges with gold braid that can be purchased at trimming counters. A very large ball can be made by inflating a balloon and then covering it over with several layers of papier-mâché — add garlands of gold beads if you want.

Another kind of ball is made of an ordinary ornament decorated with pearls or shells. Use Duco cement as the adhesive.

A String of Bells

Cut out three bells exactly alike and fold them down the center. Paste them together, and they will make a three-sided bell. Several of them pasted around a string will make a nice tree ornament or a chandelier decoration. Pine trees and stars can be made in the same way.

A Powder-Puff Clown

This expressive clown was made from a white powder puff. His features were cut from colored paper and pasted on to the puff, but you can also sew them on with bits of bright-colored woolen yarn. The cap is of glossy white paper with red peppermint-stick stripes.

From an Old Compact

Take the mirrors out of old compacts or rouge boxes and "frame" them in round cardboard mounts by cutting holes the proper size. Decorate them with cutouts. Fasten loops in the back with stickers and hang them on the Christmas tree.

21

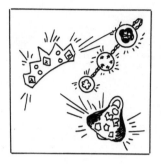

Last Year's Ornaments

If some of your tree ornaments have been broken since last year, crush them into small pieces. Cut large stars or bells from light cardboard, cover the front with paste, and sprinkle over them the bright fragments of broken balls. They make attractive tree decorations.

Old Costume Jewelry

Cut out stars, crowns, and other emblems from colored cardboard, and sew fast to them old pieces of costume jewelry. These, too, will grace the Christmas tree.

Pocketbook Mirrors

If there are some extra pocketbook mirrors around the house, let the children decorate them on both sides with cutouts from Christmas cards and bits of lace paper doilies. Use stickers to attach loops for hanging them on the tree, where they will sparkle in the light. Small children will have fun doing this — a good stormy day pastime.

Jeweled Angel

This little angel is made from a piece of costume jewelry. Make body and face of cardboard and paste on jewels with Duco cement.

6. CHRISTMAS ACTIVITIES FOR THE FAMILY

Christmas Wrappings

In the illustrations below, you see an enterprising family absorbed in making their own Christmas wrapping papers. Each member chose a symbol for himself, drew it, and then transferred it to a potato. This is the simplest kind of block printing.

The procedure is as follows: Slice a large potato in half with a sharp knife so that you have a clean cut. Draw a design on a piece of colored paper, cut it out, and put it on the potato. The moisture will make it cling. Incise around the design to the depth of one-quarter inch and cut away the background, so that the pattern will stand out in relief. Apply tempera paint with a brush to this potato block. You can use more than one color. Make your imprints on tissue or other wrapping paper of your own choosing.

The illustration on the right shows paper which will be used for wrapping gifts from the whole family. All the individual blocks were combined to make a family pattern.

Christmas Labels

Make gay, individual stickers for your packages from red and green oilcloth. Cut them into shapes appropriate for the season. If there is a pair of pinking shears in the family and no edict

against using it for oilcloth, you can make some very effective cutouts. Bright-colored felt hats that have served their time can be cut out in the same way. (See also page 146.)

On Christmas Eve

It is a pleasant custom for the family to go together in the early evening to distribute gifts to their friends. Father carries the gifts in a large decorated basket. Let the children wear costumes, and carry a minstrel lantern. Jingle a sleigh bell as the doors open, or make up a little Christmas poem or a song with which to greet your friends.

Caroling Candles

This is a beautiful old way of beginning the Christmas ceremonies. The head of the house lights a tall candle, which is the Christmas light. As he does so, he begins to sing a familiar carol. He sings one line, and passes the candle to Mother or one of the children, who also sings a line, and passes it on until the whole carol has been sung.

Jack's Afire

The person sitting nearest the fire picks up a long stick, lights it, and blows on it, saying, "Jack's afire," and passes it on to the next person. This one repeats the words, blows on the stick and quickly passes it on. The one holding it when it goes out must pay a penalty, which is to have a mustache put on his face with the charred end.

Anyone so unfortunate as to have the stick burn out in his hand a second time, gets a beard.

After the Fireside Supper

People like to sit around a fire after supper and do things which are amusing but not taxing physically or mentally. Several little forfeit games are popular at such a time. Let a guest draw a Christmas wreath on a paper napkin, stretch the napkin over the mouth of a tumbler, and make a hole in the wreath with his cigarette. Pass the tumbler around, and let everyone make a hole which touches the other one. When the center of the wreath falls out, the one who made the final hole must pay a forfeit.

Capping Marshmallows

As marshmallows are toasted, little caps form at the top. A group around the fire can have a contest over the coffee cups, removing and eating the caps as they become crisp, and seeing whose marshmallow is gone first.

25

Cutting Snowflakes

Have some extra paper napkins and several pairs of scissors at hand. Let the guests cut snowflakes, giving a prize for the best effort. If some of them have never done this before, or have forgotten some of their kindergarten tricks, show them how to fold the napkins.

Snowball Competition

Have a small tree trimmed with colored cardboard discs which have been numbered. The guests make snowballs of their paper napkins and pelt them at the discs, score is kept, and the one getting the highest score is the winner. A variation is to have a caption on each disc. It may be a "fortune" or it may tell the person who hits it to perform a stunt, or pay a penalty.

Pick-up Sticks

As a variation of jackstraws, play the old game which is its ancestor. Pile up the sticks for the fireplace, and then, in turn, try to take off one at a time without moving the others. Anyone who succeeds may have another turn, until he misses. The one who secures the greatest number of sticks in this way is, of course, the winner. This is a sit-on-the-floor game which will remove any trace of mental stiffness from the party, even if it produces some stiffness in the limbs.

Irish Potato Pancakes

The traditional Christmas Eve supper in Ireland is potato pancakes, fried
over the hearth-fire (which is the
only kind of fire most of the cottages
have). The door is always left open,
as a sign of hospitality and for good
luck while the hearth supper is being
made. The pancakes are made of
mashed potatoes thickened with flour,
seasoned, with a pinch of baking soda
added, and they may be eaten with
butter or, in truly Irish fashion, with
syrup, if that is to your taste.

Christmas Eve is a day of fasting
and abstinence in Catholic communities, and these pancakes have made
up the main dish at this meal for hundreds of years. For a party, they could
be rolled out in advance, then fried
over the hearth.

Candle Ceremony

On a table, set out as many candles as there
are people in the company. At a given time
everyone takes up a candle. The youngest
member of the family lights his candle first,
and while all sing a carol, he goes around and
lights all the other candles with his own.

BENEVOLENCE

Widen the Family Circle

Hospitality, kindness, benevolence, these as well as peace and
good will are Christmas watchwords. Adopting a family less well

off than your own, either in this world's goods or in happiness or well-being, will enrich Christmas for all of you. This calls for delicacy and tact. Choose a family as much the same as your own as possible in numbers and ages, then devise ways of making their Christmas brighter.

A Toy Repair Shop

Have the children go over their toys and decide which ones they will give away. Some of them will doubtless need repairing, so set aside an evening for this. Father may want to help on the repairs needed. Mother will probably help with the cutting and sewing of new clothes for the dolls. And even young children, if supervised, can give a fresh coat of paint here and there where needed.

People Without Families

People without families must not be forgotten. They will appreciate being invited to help decorate the tree and to join in the carol singing on Christmas Eve.

Remember Sir Launfal's vision and the revelation that was given him:

> "Not what we give, but what we share,
> For the gift without the giver is bare;
> Who gives himself with his alms feeds three —
> Himself, his hungering neighbour, and Me."

AN IMPROMPTU PLAY FOR A CHILDREN'S PARTY

An impromptu play often provides more fun than one which has been in preparation for a long time. At Christmas time, especially, there is so much dramatic subject matter in the air that it takes only a good director with an able assistant or two to do something very fine.

Here is a way of going about it which has been tried and found very effective: The leader must have several ideas in mind, but the group can choose the one they wish to dramatize. If there is a large group, divide the children into "companies" and let each group give a play, with the audience as judges.

Have a large Christmas tree of cardboard set up (see illustration.) Holes are bored all over it, and in these are placed pieces of paper twirled to make them look attractive and interesting. On each paper is the name of a character which the child who draws it is to depict.

To avoid a child's drawing a character he is obviously unfitted to portray, have difficult parts represented by certain legends like this: "You may select Santa Claus," or "the Mother," "the Fairy Godmother," etc. Children as a rule have good taste and good judgment, and in this way no feelings will be hurt.

Select subjects which call for a number of small parts. Something centering on Santa Claus can bring in the reindeer — Dasher, Dancer, Prancer, Vixen, Comet, Cupid, Donder, Blitzen. Other stock characters could be a princess, a king, Father, Mother, witch, Saint Nicholas, children, Jack Frost, etc.

When the cast has been selected, take them into an adjoining room where some simple costume accessories and props have been gathered. The children who will be the audience for the performance can sing while they are waiting, or someone can recite or play the piano.

The leader or the director appointed for the play will then explain the plot to the cast, and they will be encouraged to invent their own lines. Most children get into the spirit of dramatization very readily. If short subjects are selected and the group is not too large, perhaps everyone present can have a chance to perform.

If you wish to run it as a sort of "little theater" tournament, have two or more companies of the children give a play with the same plot, but with dialogue and business differing according to the ideas and tastes of the participants. Have a jury to decide which is the better or best.

A Candle Trick

Extinguish a candle — preferably a good-sized one which will make a thick curl of smoke. Hold a lighted match to the smoke two or three inches away from the candle. The fire will run down the smoke trail and relight the candle.

Egg Magic

Mother won't like the idea of egg magic at her dinner table, but try it out first in the kitchen and convince her that it can be done. Stand two egg cups side by side several inches apart. Put an egg (uncooked) in one of them. Blow the egg with a strong, steady breath, and it will leap from one egg cup to the other. Your guests will like this trick.

Tree Puzzle

Cut a piece of thin wood about four inches long and three-quarters of an inch wide. Make three holes, as shown here. String two leather trees, acorns, cranberries, beads, or anything else appropriate on a piece of twine twelve or fourteen inches long and then hang them from the wooden block in the manner illustrated. The puzzle is to get the trees (or whatever else it may be) upon the same loop. This is how it is done: Draw tree A along the string through loop B at the center hole; then pull the loop through the hole and pass the tree through the two loops which will result from this procedure. Draw the string back through the hole as before and tree A can be easily passed over to join the other one.

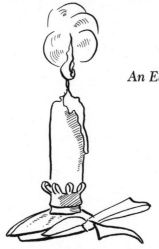

An Edible Candle

Cut a piece of apple to resemble a candle and into it stick an unsalted almond. The almond wick can be lighted and it will burn for a minute or two, after which the whole "candle" can be eaten in the presence of the company.

A Revolving Tree

Cut a piece of cardboard in a long spiral. Make a stand of a block of wood with a dowel stick glued into the center of it (you will, of course have to bore a hole in the block.) Put a needle at the upper end of the dowel, then place the spiral on its point, as shown in the picture. Set the stand on a radiator and the spiral will revolve.

To Balance a Stick on the End of a Glass of Water

Take a stick about a foot long and two penknives of equal weight, size, and shape. Stick the knives by the points, about three inches from one end of the wood and exactly opposite each other. Now fill a goblet with water, and rest the end of the stick on one side. If the knife handles are curved, the curves must be turned in toward the goblet. Now you can drink the contents of the goblet and the stick will remain just as you have placed it. If you make sure that the knives are perfectly balanced, the trick is bound to be successful. Again, we recommend trying it in the kitchen first.

32

A Trick Tree

Six pieces of newspaper, wrapping paper, or lightweight construction paper must be rolled into a tight tube to make one of these trees. The cubelike figure above shows the six pieces of paper and the drawing underneath the tube. Tear or cut slashes through all thicknesses  to within about two inches of the bottom. Gently pull the center piece upward, allowing the tube to turn slowly as the slashed ends emerge spiral fashion. These make effective table or room decorations. You can put them in flower pots or bowls to look like tree formations, shrubs, etc.

PLANS FOR A CRÈCHE

The Children Can Make This Crèche

This Nativity scene is made entirely from cardboard. It can be any size. The figures are so simple that it is not difficult to enlarge them. Cut around the outside lines of the figures and fold back the little pieces to make them stand up. Color them with poster paints. Make the inside lines strong to indicate the flow of the garments and the features.

For the manger, use a rectangular piece of cardboard, and follow exactly the directions on the sketch. Cut on the heavy lines, fold on the broken lines. The cradle is made of a square piece of cardboard. When you have cut the heavy lines and made the folds along the dotted lines, paste A over B, on the angle, as in the drawing, with C underneath. Make the infant's head of a piece of silk or nylon cloth, stuff with cotton, and paint on features.

Put the crèche on a table with some of the branches from the Christmas tree around it and two lighted candles. The children will enjoy making it, and they can use it for a setting when they dramatize some of the Christmas carols, as suggested elsewhere in this book.

The Children Can Entertain with a Puppet Play

You have made the crèche, we hope, and to make these animal puppets will be the work of only a half hour or so. Then you can give a play for the family and the friends who are with you on Christmas Day. It is certain that a "return engagement" will be requested a number of times during the holidays.

Trace the animals — the donkey, the cow, and the sheep — on cardboard or construction paper, and color them to fit the descriptions in the poem "The Friendly Beasts," on page 38. Make them into rod puppets by attaching small wooden dowels or sticks. Fasten one stick in the middle of the back and one behind the neck, for holding and manipulating. The heads of the animals can be made separately and attached so they will move as the animal speaks. Bore a hole in the body and one in the neck and attach with a brass paper fastener.

For a puppet stage, use a card table hung around with a curtain. Put the crèche on the table, and hold the rod puppets near it as they "speak." That is one of the legends of Christmas, you know, that the animals are given the gift of speech on Christmas Eve because they shared their stable with the Christ child.

Three children can take part in the play, or two can do it by assuming different voices. A background of music would add to it, or perhaps all would join in singing a Christmas carol.

THE FRIENDLY BEASTS

12th Century English

1. Je - sus our broth - er kind and good, Was
2. "I," said the don - key shag-gy and brown, "I,

hum - bly born in a sta - ble rude, And the
car-ried His moth - er up-hill and down; I

friend - ly beasts a - round Him stood;
car-ried His moth-er to Beth-le-hem town."

Je - sus our broth - er kind and good.
"I," said the don - key shag-gy and brown.

3. "I," said the cow, all white and red,
   "I gave Him my manger for His bed,
   I gave Him my hay to pillow His head."
   "I," said the cow, all white and red.

4. "I," said the sheep, with curly horn,
   "I gave Him my wool for His blanket warm;
   He wore my coat on Christmas morn,"
   "I," said the sheep, with curly horn.

5. "I," said the dove, from my rafter high,
   "Cooed Him to sleep that He should not cry,
   We cooed Him to sleep, my mate and I,"
   "I," said the dove, from my rafter high.

6. And every beast, by some good spell,
   In the stable dark, was glad to tell
   Of the gift he gave Immanuel,
   The gift he gave Immanuel.

(See page 36 for directions for making a puppet play of this beautiful old carol.)

Santa Pillow Puppet

This little Santa Claus puppet rests on top of a pillow which is used for a stage. Make the body and head out of heavy cardboard, and just below the shoulders, cut two armholes at points a child's forefinger and thumb can be thrust through comfortably to form the arms. Paint on Santa's face with colored paints and then cover the body with red cloth; also make a red cap for the top of his head. For trimming on the suit and white beard, use cotton or white wool yarn. Make sleeves of the same material as the body for covering the fingers so that the arms will be more realistic.

The puppet's body can move up and down and its arms can gesture. It is possible to have Santa point his finger, pick up toys from the pillow, etc. If several children are playing, let them make other characters so they can converse back and forth.

A Pomander for Mother. The most attractive pomander balls are made from oranges, but very small children can make them from apples. Whole cloves are pushed into the fruit; they must be very close together completely covering it. The cloves mingled with the fruit give a pleasant, spicy scent. Thread colored twine through the center of the fruit for hanging it up, or make tarlatan bags with a drawstring and put the orange or apple inside.

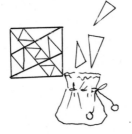

A Puzzle for Father. From a piece of thin cardboard cut ten square pieces of equal size. Then cut each of the squares in two on the diagonal and you will have twenty triangles. Put these in a bag and slip it in among Father's gifts, with a note telling him to make a perfect square out of all the triangles, if he can. Use red cardboard and a green bag, or the other way around.

A Christmas Tree for the Birds. A tiny cedar tree, a lopped off branch of a Christmas tree, or an artificial tree from the ten-cent store will help to give the birds in your neighborhood a happy holiday season. Decorate the tree with cranberries, strings of popcorn, and small cubes of suet tied on with varicolored yarn. Put it on the porch or on a window sill and there will be a great coming and going of singing guests.

7. GAMES FOR CHILDREN'S PARTIES

Marching to the Christmas Tree. No matter how many Christmas trees the children see during the holidays, a new one is always an event, especially the one they all look forward to seeing at their holiday party in their own home or community center. Take advantage, therefore, of this factor, and instead of receiving them in the main room where the party is to be held, have them meet in another place and get your party off to a dramatic start by having them march to find the Christmas tree. Let one of the boys be dressed as a drummer, with gay sash and paper hat. He is in on the secret, of course, and beating his drum, he leads them into and around several bare rooms — bare, that is, in the party sense — and finally he takes them into the room where the tree is set up.

A Chalk Talk. To vary the hilarious activities of the children's Christmas party, and to give a necessary breathing spell, let the children give a chalk talk. Have an easel or piece of beaverboard on which can be tacked pieces of wrapping or construction paper. Have colored chalks and crayons and let each child have a turn giving an impromptu talk. He may draw pictures of what he received for Christmas, tell a story, or anything else appropriate. This is a good way to draw out the shy members of the group.

Christmas Lotto. A good pencil-and-paper game for an interim of sitting down between active games is Christmas lotto. Draw twenty-five squares on as many pieces of paper as you'll need. Choose a variety of toys from a list of seventy-five and write their names in the squares, allowing one square for each toy. Make sure that no piece of paper is exactly like another. The leader reads from the list of seventy-five toys (no repetitions, of course), and as a child hears the name of a toy that is on his paper, he crosses out that square. The first one to cross out a whole line of five, either on the straight or the diagonal, cries "Lotto" and wins that round.

Name That Toy. Have a large paper sack decorated to represent Santa Claus's pack, and put twelve toys in it. The contents of the bag must be varied according to the ages of the children who are taking part in the game. Give each child pencil and paper and let all write down what they think the pack contains, then give a prize to the one making the nearest guess.

This game can be varied by asking the children to be seated in a circle and passing each one a large Christmas stocking. Next, blindfold them and announce Santa will put a toy in each stocking if they will hold it out in front of them. The object of the game is to guess the name of the toy by pressing in on the stocking to feel its shape. The first to guess will have the next turn at being Santa Claus. The game can be varied by substituting different shaped fruits or nuts for the toys, or it may be used as a novel way to distribute gifts.

Follow the Leader Games. Seat the children in a circle and let them enjoy a follow-the-leader game. The group leader can pantomime a character or a Christmas activity, and they must all imitate the actions. Or a story may be acted out such as eating turkey, trimming a tree, etc., and then the children can guess what it is. Each child can be given a turn as the leader in the middle of the circle.

Christmas Ship. This is a pantomime game designed to make the children laugh. The children are seated in a circle and one child starts the game by saying to his neighbor:

"My Christmas ship came in."

"What did it bring you?" asks the next child.

"A dog," says the first child, and begins barking.

The second child in turn must also play at being a dog, and then say to his neighbor, "My Christmas ship came in," dramatizing his gift with actions or sound. If the children are old enough, they should dramatize every gift named, before naming their own, but this would be difficult for tots to remember. By the time a few dogs are barking, two or three trains are steaming around the room, the game will have broken the ice.

Ribbon Game. Each person in the group takes a ribbon and holds it by one end. The ribbons (or tape) must be of equal length. The other ends are all united in the hands of the one who leads the game and who is, therefore, placed in the middle of the circle. When the leader says, "Pull," they must all let go; when he says, "Let go," each one must pull on the ribbon which he is holding. The object is for the leader to confuse the players into doing what he orders, and for the players to do just the opposite. Any player who obeys the leader or who drops his ribbon at the wrong time is out.

Santa Claus Crossing the Ice. This is a Christmas version of an obstacle race, and is hilarious for a large group. Divide the guests into two groups and ask them to take their places on opposite sides of the room. Two lines of obstacles are set up between the groups, running north and south of the room, that is, if the guests happen to be seated east and west. The obstacles must be the same in both lines. Each side chooses two representatives — Santa Claus and his reindeer guide. They have the responsibility of either winning or losing for their respective sides. There is only one chance in this game. Each reindeer tries to lead his Santa, who is blindfolded, safely from one end of the obstacle line to the other by jingling a sleigh bell. A sharp, loud, note means "danger," and soft tones indicate "straight ahead."

Gift-Carrying Contest. Ask the children to form a large circle and place a Christmas package on each child's head. They must then march around the room to music; the contest is to see which one can manage to keep the gift on his head the longest. This child should receive a second gift as a reward.

A variation of the game is to give each child a knife on which are several holly berries to keep intact while marching. If older children are playing the game, start and stop the music suddenly once in a while to break the rhythm.

Observation Game. Each player is given a card listing a dozen objects previously placed in the room. They are not hidden, but laid in inconspicuous positions where a person will be able to see them if he should glance in the right direction. For instance, a one-dollar bill can be stretched around the back of a green book, a gold star pasted on a gold decoration, a red rubber band on the top of a lamp base, etc. The players remain seated, and note the position of the objects on their card.

Bubble Game. Children love to blow bubbles, so why not let them vie for Christmas presents at a party? When a bubble alights on a package, it belongs to the person who blew it.

Christmas Snowballs. Make balls out of cotton and then cover the outside with white tissue paper. They can be made to look more realistic by applying spots of mucilage and sifting on frost powder or artificial snow. They can be batted around the room for a snowball fight, or you can have a relay race.

Snowball Relay. Divide the children into equal groups and stand them in line, one behind the other. In front of each line, but on opposite side of the room, place a chair on which is an empty box or basket. The snowballs are dropped on the carpet in a long line stretching from the basket to the children; at a given signal, the first child in each line picks up the balls, one at a time, and puts them in the basket. He then returns, taps the second child, and goes to the back of the line. The second child takes the balls out of the basket, one by one, and puts them back on the floor in a straight line ready for the third child to pick up. The contest is to see which team can finish first.

Holly and Mistletoe. Divide the children into two teams and give the holly team a large red stocking and the mistletoe team a green one. Hang them in opposite ends of a room where previously have been concealed many pieces of candy, some wrapped in red paper and some, in green. The players form in line, red and green alternating, and they begin marching to a lively tune such as "Jingle Bells." When the music stops very suddenly, all break ranks and try to find their own color candy, then drop them one at a time into their team's stocking. When the music resumes, the players form in line again and so on until the game ends.

A Basket of Greens. This game is designed for children who are old enough to identify different varieties of Christmas greens. Make

it more complicated for adults by mixing in as many species of evergreens, spruce, hemlock, etc. as you can find and see if they can name them according to the grouping of the needles.

8. OLD CHRISTMAS GAMES

Post and Pair

This was a highly popular card game during early English Christmas parties. Ben Johnson alluded to it in his "Masque of Christmas":
> "Now Post and Pair, old Christmas's heir
> Doth make a gingling sally;
> And wot you who, 'tis one of my two
> Sons, card makers in Pur Alley."

It was played thus: Three cards were dealt to all, the excitement of the game consisting in each of the young people vying or betting, on the goodness of his own hand. A pair of royal aces was the best hand, the next any other three cards of a kind according to their orders. If there were no threes, the highest pairs would win.

The Game of Goose

(This is a game reported by Joseph Strutt in his famous book, long out of print, *Sports and Pastimes of the People of England.*" The first edition of this work was printed in London in 1801.)

"We have a childish diversion usually introduced at Christmas time, called the Game of Goose. This game may be played by two persons; but it will readily admit of many more; it is well calculated to make children ready at reckoning the produce of two given numbers. The table for playing at goose is usually an impression from a copper-plate pasted upon a cartoon about the size of a sheet almanack, and divided into sixty-two small compartments . . . with a large open space in the midst marked with the number sixty-three; the lesser compartments have singly an appropriate number from one to sixty-two inclusive, beginning at the outmost extremity of the spiral lines. At the commencement of the play, everyone of the competitors puts a stake into the space at No. 63. There are also different forfeitures in the course of the game that are added, and the whole belongs to the winner. At No. 5 is a bridge which claims a forfeit in passing; at 19 an alehouse where you pay for washing; at 42 a labyrinth which carries you back to 23; at 51 the prison where you must rest until relieved by another casting the same throw; at 58 the grave whence you begin the game again; and at 61 the goblet where you pay for tasting. The game is played with two dice, and every player throws in his turn as he sits at the table; he must have a counter or some other small mark which he can distinguish from the marks of his antagonists, and according to the amount of the two numbers thrown upon the dice he places his mark; that is to say, if he throws a four and a five, which amounts to nine, he places his mark at nine upon the table, moving it the next throw as many numbers forward as the dice permit him, and so on until the game be completed, namely when the number sixty-three is made exactly; all above it the player reckons back, and then throws again in his turn. If the second thrower at the beginning of the game casts the same number as the first, he takes up his piece, and the first player is obliged to begin the game again. If the same thing happens in the middle of the game, the first player goes back to the place he last came from. It is called the game of goose, because at every fourth and fifth compartment in succession a goose is depicted, and if the cast thrown by the player falls upon a goose, he moves forward double the number of his throw."

THE GAME OF GOOSE

9. NOVEL WAYS OF DISTRIBUTING THE CHRISTMAS GIFTS

A Christmas Crown

The Christmas crown is a jolly way of distributing gifts and it makes a lovely decoration, as well. It is a part of the Swedish Christmas tradition. Use a large wooden hoop, or make one of wire. Cover the frame with colored muslin or paper, and decorate it with tinsel and greens, making it as gay as you possibly can. Tie the Christmas packages to it by long ribbons (the contents can't be too heavy, of course) and suspend the hoop from the ceiling by long, stout ropes. Colored popcorn balls can be hung between the packages. The crown is hung so that it can be made to whirl, and while it is going round, the guests grab for packages. Sometimes two or three at a time are blindfolded, and try to catch a gift as the crown whirls around, while the others look on, awaiting their turns.

Perhaps the most important family gift is one that is too large to be included around the tree, or you may wish to make it appear more important than the others. It is easy to screw a small metal hook into the ceiling, just over the spot where the object is to be placed and tie onto it a dark-colored string or picture wire to which a small decorated tree is attached, as shown in the drawing.

This is a divided tree — half masculine and half for "my lade." This idea calls for unusual decorations which should appeal to anyone who likes to be creative or original. Of course, it can also be divided horizontally, decorating the top for adults and the lower part for children. In this case, allow the children to make and hang their own ornaments.

51

Santa Claus is, of course, the proper person to distribute the gifts at a children's party. If he should appear as a buffoon, bringing Mrs. Santa with him, it would greatly add to the merriment of the occasion. Grownups like buffoons, too, for they are at the same time naïve and sophisticated.

It is easy to improvise a buffoon stage, and the figures are simple to make. A regular buffoon stage resembles a large blackboard frame with a little platform extending beyond the frame. The person or persons manipulating the buffoons stand behind a black (or dark) curtain which hangs on the frame. There are slits in the curtain, one for the head of the manipulator and two for his hands. He holds the puppet figure so that his own head appears to be attached to it. If you haven't a suitable frame, suspend an "apron" across a doorway with a table beneath it. The sleeves of the puppet's suit are wide and empty, and the manipulator sticks his hands through these. He makes the figures walk

and dance by pulling a string which is attached to the knees of the figure by a ring.

To make the buffoons, use muslin for the body and legs and cotton batting or rags for stuffing. Make a good-sized doll — a large, broad rectangle for the top, a smaller one for the bottom, and stuffed legs. In dressing the figures, be sure to have the arm-holes wide enough for the performer's hands to go through. The clothes are not sewed up in the back. Have some sort of ruff or neck trimming. The manipulator wears the headdress on his own head.

The performers must have ready tongues and be able to keep up a flow of small talk. Santa Claus and Mrs. Santa could lead the assembly in singing Christmas songs before distributing the presents, or this part of the program could end with group singing.

The children will enjoy using the stage all during the party, doing some dramatics — even if it is only reciting nursery rhymes. Finally, everyone will stick their heads through to have a picture taken if someone happens to have a camera.

10. CHRISTMAS ICE-BREAKER

There is a tale of an old knight who invited all his tenants to his castle on Christmas Eve for a holiday feast. Just as they were assembled around the table, he had them pause until he offered a toast:

" 'Now, let no man eat or drinke until he who is master over his wife shall sing a lusty carroll.'

"There were uneasy glances about the room, and finally a shy man rose and sang a few words of an old carol, but he sat down suddenly, as though under an unseen influence.

"Then said the knight, 'Let no woman eat or drinke until she who is master over her husband shall sing a carroll.'

"Whereupon the whole assemblage of women fell to such a singing that there was never heard such a catterwalling piece of musicke. Whereat the knight laughed so heartily, that it did him halfe as much good as a corner of his Christmas pie."

Hodening

This game is adapted from an old British holiday custom. A character wearing a grotesque mask resembling a horse's head would look in the window and clank its teeth. After giving the family a good scare, it expected to be invited in for a treat of cakes and cider.

In Wales it was the custom for the hodening horse to recite long extemporaneous poems, whereupon the host returned other extemporaneous poems; if the disguised horse could outwit the host, he gained admittance. By having two masks, you might develop this idea further by playing the old game of challenges, in which each tries to outdo the other, as in a spelling bee.

54

11. TRADITIONAL CHRISTMAS FOODS

Christmas fare has always varied in different locations, but everywhere there has been sentiment for certain foods, arising sometimes from religious associations or because of some provincial circumstance, as in the case of our own turkey, which the Indians introduced to the early colonists to enhance their scanty board.

In feudal England the boar's head, a "baron of beef," a haunch of venison, and even peacock were on the Christmas table. There was another stand-by called "plum pottage," or "plum broth," which was the invariable first course for several hundred years. This dish was made of beef or mutton stewed slowly and thickened with brown bread. When the meat was about half tender, raisins, currants, prunes, cloves, mace, and ginger were added, and then it simmered for another hour or so. We may judge how important it was when we recall that Sir Roger de Coverley made the statement that he thought there was some hope for a Dissenter when he saw him enjoy this porridge on Christmas Eve or Christmas Day.

Whatever is the main course of your Christmas dinner — turkey, goose, ham, etc. — you must have a plum pudding, for that has become well established as the fitting dessert. King Arthur himself made one, and his recipe has come down to us, although the proportions are rather vague according to present ideas of scientific cookery:

"A bag pudding the king did make
And stuffed it well with plums;
And in it put great lumps of fat
As big as my two thumbs."

The record says that he put in three bags of barley meal, and they were probably of considerable size, since the king, his queen, and the whole court did "eat thereof," and there was some left over, which "was not thrown away."

Here are two excellent recipes for plum pudding, and one for an excellent sauce. Of course you know that the plum pudding should be served with ceremony. When the table has been cleared, and all sit expectantly, it should be brought to the table lighted. Brandy or other spirits — West Indian rum does very well — must be poured over the pudding and then, at the touch of a match, blue flames will leap around it.

English Plum Pudding

Mix 1 pound of chopped suet, ½ pound of brown sugar, ¾ pound of stale bread crumbs, and ¼ pound of flour. Add 5 eggs, 1 teacupful of sweet cider, the juice and grated rind of 1 lemon, 1 pound of currants, 1 pound of raisins, ½ pound of minced candied orange peel, and about half a grated nutmeg. When well blended, turn the mixture into a buttered mold with a cover, and steam it for 7 or 8 hours. Garnish with holly and serve with hard sauce.

Individual Plum Pudding

Shred and chop ½ pound of suet, pick over and wash ½ pound of raisins. Put the suet in a bowl, add 1 teacupful of New Orleans molasses, 1 teacupful of sour cream, 1 teaspoon of soda dissolved in the cream, 1 tablespoon of cinnamon, ½ teaspoon of cloves, and ⅓ teaspoon of allspice. Stir in 3 teacupfuls of flour which has been sifted with 1 teaspoon of baking powder. Beat vigorously, add the raisins, which should be lightly dusted with flour, and turn into individual buttered molds. Steam for 1½ hours.

Sunshine Sauce

Beat ¼ pound of butter and ½ cup of sugar together until light, then add the yolks of 6 eggs beaten to a cream. Scald 1 pint of cream in the double boiler, add slowly to the egg mixture, and cook for 10 minutes in the double boiler over low heat. Remove from fire, add ¼ teaspoon of salt, and the sauce is ready to serve.

An Old Fruit Cake Recipe

Two cups white sugar, 1 cup butter, 1 cup of New Orleans molasses, 5 eggs, 1 cup sour milk, 5 cups flour, 1 pound raisins, 1 pound currants, 1 pound citron and 1 pound dates. Flour the raisins, currants, citron, and dates before putting them into the batter which has been made first. One teaspoon of soda in hot water, 1 tablespoon of cinnamon, 1 tablespoon each of cloves and nutmeg, ½ cup of blackberry jelly stirred into the batter. Bake for 2 hours in a moderately hot oven.

Cranberry Juice

Cranberry growers now have two types of juice on the market which are excellent for making punch or nonalcoholic drinks during the holiday season. One is called "cranberry cocktail," which can be mixed with club soda or ginger ale and any other fruit juice you wish to include. The other is Cram — a concentrated juice which, when mixed with any of the sparkling waters, is a delicious drink "on the rocks."

The Christmas Commissary

Staples cannot be dispensed with even at holiday time, but there must always be a few special foods that look different and have some special flavor to distinguish them from ordinary, round-the-year fare.

Rosemary Christmas Broth

From Georgia comes this interesting recipe. Weaver Dallas has an old family soup tureen. For the buffet supper on Christmas night, when all her friends may drop in, she serves this traditional rosemary Christmas broth from it.

> 1 quart chicken stock
> 1 quart beef stock
> 1 quart stock from pigs' feet

In preparing the chicken stock, put in 1 teaspoon chopped parsley, 1 teaspoon onion, and a pinch of pepper. In the beef stock, bay leaf, a pinch of thyme, a little basil and sweet marjoram. With the pigs' feet, put in a good dash of nutmeg. Strain the three stocks through a colander, add a quart of tomato juice (or more, if you like). Then give a final seasoning of herbs. Put in one sprig of rosemary — only one, because it is strong — and one garlic clove. Let them stay for a few minutes, but do not cook them in the broth. Take them out, reheat the broth, pour it into a tureen decorated with rosemary around the rim, and serve in bouillon cups. With beaten biscuit and sandwiches, it makes a delectable main course for a buffet supper at night after a rich holiday dinner.

It is possible to make rosemary Christmas broth with prepared bouillon cubes and powders if the original method puts too much strain on your time and household facilities. They come in chicken and beef flavors, and are a good substitute for home-made stock. It is not necessary to have the pigs' feet stock if it seems too difficult. There is no powder or cube on the market that simulates this flavor. When using the prepared broth foundation, follow the directions exactly as given above.

Colored Sugar Decoration

Almonds and other kinds of nutmeats look attractive and really merit the name "sweetmeats" when coated with colored sugar. It is a very simple process.

Take one cup of granulated sugar and seven tablespoons of water and cook until the mixture is just about to turn to sugar again. Color it with a few drops of vegetable dye and flavor with mint, wintergreen, or whatever pleases you. While the mixture is still hot, drop in the nutmeats. Take them out at once and lay them on waxed paper.

Grapefruit rind can be coated in the same way. If you like it soft, cook it first until transparent and dip it in the sugar mixture. If you prefer it hard, dry it out and then dip it.

Peppernuts

Use any kind of cookie dough. Roll it out in long, round pieces about an inch in diameter and cut cookies on the diagonal. Sprinkle with cinnamon, and, if you like, finely ground nuts, before baking.

A Holly Wreath Salad

Use chicory and put it on the salad plates in the shape of a wreath. Put cranberries or cherries here and there, to resemble holly.

Snowball Salad

Thicken cranberry juice with gelatin. Put it either into individual molds or into a large mold, then garnish it with balls of cream cheese.

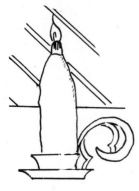

A Candle Salad

Roll a banana in red or green sugar. Set it, upright, into a ring of pineapple or a cross section of an apple for a holder. Split an almond (unsalted, or with the salt rubbed off) and stick the pieces into the top of the banana. Light the almond just before serving. It will burn for a minute or two.

Egg Nog Sauce for Holiday Puddings

Separate 3 eggs, beat the whites stiff, and set them aside. Beat the yolks, add the whites and 3 tablespoons of sugar, and beat some more. Then add any flavoring you like — 1 teaspoon of rum, or 2 teaspoons of whisky.

A Christmas Confection

For children's parties, soften oranges by rolling them, and cut a small round hole at the top of each; then insert a stick of peppermint candy. The children will enjoy sucking the juice of the orange through the sticks. Country children used to do this with lemon sticks.

Christmas Beverage

Have a beverage bar rigged up as part of the room decoration. Put vegetable dye in the water before freezing it for ice cubes. If you want to make them especially ornamental, freeze holly leaves or little Christmas bells in the cubes. To do this, partially freeze the water, and then put in your tokens. They will remain in the middle of the cubes.

A Beverage for Children

For nursery-age children or just post-nursery, make a drink with milk, a spoonful of ice cream, and color with vegetable dye — pink, you will find, is the favorite color — then sprinkle the top with colored sugar.

Spiced Cider

In 1 quart of sweet cider put ½ cup of sugar, 8 short sticks of cinnamon, 12 whole cloves, and a little allspice, also a pinch of salt. Heat to the boiling point. Let stand for several hours. Reheat before serving.

Up and Coming

One pint cream, ½ cup milk, and ½ cup sweet cider are the base for this drink. Add ½ cup sugar, ½ teaspoon of vanilla, and a little nutmeg. Mix and chill.

Scalloped Oysters for Christmas Eve

Drain a pint of oysters. Mix 6 tablespoons of cream with oyster liquor, 1¼ cups of cracker or bread crumbs or mixed crumbs, and ½ cup melted butter.

Use only two layers of oysters and three of crumbs. Butter an ovenproof dish (*or* "deep casserole"), and cover the bottom with the crumb mixture; add a layer of oysters, seasoned with salt and paprika, chopped green pepper, and celery. Add successive layers of crumbs, oysters and seasonings, and, lastly, crumbs. Top with extra butter and bake in hot oven twenty minues. Serves four people.

Cookie Bar

A cookie bar for a Christmas tea party. Paste cookies to lace paper doilies with a paste made of powdered sugar and water. The doilie will serve as a tea plate. Display cookies by hanging them up and letting each guest make his own selection. See illustration on page 62.

Gilding the Cookies

A part of the Christmas fun, particularly for the children, is to add gay Christmas decorations to cookies after they are baked. It is possible to buy cutters in the usual shapes such as a tree, Santa Claus, or animals, but it is very easy to make ones of your own out of tin strips bent into various shapes. Hold them in place by soldering (you can buy liquid solder at the hardware store) onto a top cut from a tin can. Another idea is to cut out rings of dough with a doughnut cutter and decorate to resemble a Christmas wreath.

The decorative material is made by beating up an egg white and adding powdered sugar until the mixture becomes a paste. It is colored by placing small portions in individual cups and adding standard food coloring, which comes in paste forms. Use a thin paste for outline work, fine lines and dots, and a thicker, or stiffer, paste for the main object on the cookies. You may find it is necessary to add a bit of glycerine to prevent undue drying.

Gilding tools can be purchased in household departments, but it is more fun to improvise your own if you are gilding for amusement. Any pointed instrument such as an orange stick, file, or toothpick can be used for adding lines and small features. Children will enjoy using small plastic hors d'ouvres sticks with different decorative objects at the top for handles.

Decorating Sugar Cubes

Small Christmas motifs, such as holly, Christmas trees, or bells can be added to cubes of sugar in the same manner as on cookies. Note that loaf sugar comes in different grades of hardness, and select the hardest you can find. A box of decorated sugar cubes is an excellent informal Christmas gift.

DECORATIONS FOR CHRISTMAS COOKIES

12. LET US SING OUR ROUNDELAYS

So now has come our joyful'st feast
    Let every man be jolly,
Each room with ivy leaves is dressed,
And every post with holly.
    Though some churls at our mirth repine
    Round your foreheads garlands twine,
    Down sorrow in a cup of wine,
And let us all be merry.

Now all our neighbor's chimneys smoke,
And Christmas blocks are burning;
The ovens they with baked meats choke,
And all their spits are turning.
    Without the door let sorrow lie,
    And if for cold it hap to die,
    We'll bury it in a Christmas pie,
And evermore be merry.

Now every lad is wondrous trim,
And no man minds his labor;
Our lasses have provided them
A bagpipe and a tabor.
    Young men, and maids, and girls and boys,
    Give life to one another's joys,
    And you anon shall by their noise
Perceive that they are merry.

Then wherefore in these merry days
Should we, I pray, be duller?
No; let us sing our roundelays
To make out mirth the fuller.
    And, whilst thus inspired we sing,
    Let us all the streets with echoes ring;
    Woods, and hills, and everything,
Bear witness we are merry.

                GEORGE WITHER *(1588-1667)*

13. CHRISTMAS ENTERTAINMENT FOR GROUPS

The Yule Log

The ancient yule log ceremony, complete with log hunt in a snow-covered forest and drinking wassail by an open fire, is a favorite Christmas celebration in our northern states. The choppers meet on the village square, and after a round of carol singing, they head for the woods to search for the yule log, which was notched and hidden there weeks before. The discoverers haul it to its destination with great pomp and ceremony, where it is lighted with a brand saved from the year before. The log is highly decorated with greens and bright-colored ribbons, and the youngest child rides atop as it is being hauled from the woods.

Among ceremonies used for lighting the yule log is one in which the youngest child in the home pours wine on the log while the father offers a prayer that the fire might warm the cold, that the hungry might gain food, that the weary find rest, and that all enjoy heaven's peace.

Another moving ceremony is one where all guests are assembled, and as the yule log approaches, the entire company begins to sing the old song written by Robert Herrick:

"Come bring, with a noise,
   My merrie, merrie boys
   The Christmas log to the firing;
While my good dame, she
   Bids ye all be free,
   And drink to your heart's desiring.
With last year's Brand
   Light the new Block, and
   For good success in his spending,
On your psalters play
   That sweet luck may
   Come while the log is aburning."

Then the host rises, and holding high his cup, he shouts so all can hear, "This yule log burns. It destroys all hatreds and misunderstandings. Let your envies banish, and let the spirit of good fellowship reign supreme for this season and through all the year."

The Wassail Bowl

After the yule log is lighted, the fireplace becomes the focal point for most of the Christmas activities with guests making merry by drinking wassail and singing carols. The wassail bowl is first paraded around the room and then set in front of the fire, where it is kept warm.

One can find many recipes for making wassail (you will find one used in Old Williamsburg elsewhere in this book), but in general the base is ale to which nutmeg, ginger, cinnamon, and lemon peel have been added. In some parts of England a bottle of sherry is added. At Lake Palmer, Wyoming, where the whole community takes part in hunting the yule log, the guests partake of a wassail made of sweet cider to which the spices, apples, and sugar have been added. The mixture is allowed to simmer (not boil), and when the sugar has dissolved, the liquid is poured into a bowl and pieces of bread are

floated on top with a few cooked apples. Wassail is often referred to as "lamb's wool" because of the old English custom of breaking into it white bread and pieces of apples so well cooked they are about to fall apart.

It was also the custom to tie apples on to long strings and then attach them at the top of the fireplace so they would be suspended above the wassail bowl. As the apples roasted in front of the fire, their juice would drip down into the warm drink.

The wassail bowl was always decorated with standing sprays of evergreens when it was being paraded around the room, then stripped of the greenery as it was placed in front of the fire. If you have no fireplace, allow the decoration to remain throughout the party.

Wassail Song

Wassail, wassail, all over the town;
Our bread it is white and our ale — it is brown.
Our bowl, it is made of the white maple tree;
With the wassailing bowl we will drink unto Thee!

Then here's to the horse, and to his right eye!
May God send our master a Good Christmas pie,
A good Christmas pie that may we all see!
With the wassailing bowl we'll drink unto Thee!

GLOUCESTERSHIRE CAROL

A "Jingle Bells" Singing Theme

A singing game is a splendid mixer for a children's party and a jolly "free-for-all" for grownups and children. This one is done to the tune of "Jingle Bells," with everyone singing as they dance. Any number of couples can take part. The partners face each other, the boys and men in one line, girls and women in the opposite. Begin with the chorus, all singing.

Chorus:

4 counts .... Walk to partner

4 counts .... Walk back

8 counts .... Walk to partner and pass through (right shoulder)

Verses: 16 counts

Head couple leads the rows down center of formation. Head couple stops at end of row, forming arch under which all couples pass. After passing under arch, couples separate and go back to original line formation. Repeat.

A *"Jingle Bells" Singing Game*

Dashing through the snow,
In a one-horse open sleigh,
O'er the fields we go,
Laughing all the way;
Bells on Bobtail ring;
Making spirits bright,
What fun it is to ride and sing
A sleighing song tonight!

Chorus:
Jingle bells, jingle bells,
Jingle all the way,
Oh, what fun it is to ride
In a one-horse open sleigh!

A day or two ago,
I thought I'd take a ride,
And soon Miss Fannie Bright
Was seated at my side.
The horse was lean and lank;
Misfortune seemed his lot,
He got into a drifted bank
And so we got upsot!

Now the ground is white,
So go it while you're young;
Take the girls tonight
And sing this sleighing song;
Just get a bob-tailed bay,
Two-forty for his speed,
Then hitch him to an open sleigh
And Crack! you'll take the lead!

Jingle Bells — I

Formation: Single circle facing in.
   "Dashing through the snow . . ."
1) All take four steps in toward center of circle
    (clap on fourth count).
2) All take four steps out from center of circle
    (clap on fourth count).
3) and (4). Repeat (1) and (2).
   "Bells on Bobtail ring . . ."
1) All slide right four counts, jumping to face outside on fourth
    count.

69

2) All slide left four counts, jumping to face inside on fourth count.

3) and (4). Swing partner around.

   Chorus: "Jingle bells, jingle bells . . ."

1) Grand right and left.

   For a prize dance, use small jingle bells, passing them during grand right and left. The one who is holding the bells at the end of the dance receives a prize.

Jingle Bells – II

Formation: Double circle.

1) Slide facing partner – one on outside right – inside left (8 measures).

2) Grasp partner's hands – fast turn in center – tiny steps (8 measures).

3) Squat down – extend right leg backward.
   Jump together – extend left leg backward.
   Jump together – extend left leg front (6 counts).

4) Four steps clockwise, side by side.

5) Face partner, walk four steps back.

6) Point diagonally to own right and walk forward four steps (meeting new partner).

7) Circle four steps with new partner. Repeat (4), (5), (6), (7).

TEACHERS' COLLEGE, COLUMBIA UNIVERSITY DANCE WORKSHOP

A Christmas Round

E. Nesbitt

1. Christ-mas is com-ing! The goose is get-ting fat;

2. Please to put a pen-ny in the old man's hat,

3. Please to put a pen-ny in the old man's hat.

Christmas Walk

A Pantomime in Four Parts for Children

This pantomime is suggested for small children to perform at school or church parties. Since the walk is based on "rhythm," the result will depend on careful selection of music for the pantomime. Many Christmas tunes such as "Jingle Bells," "The Skater's Waltz," and "Deck the Halls" can be used.

The children should be dressed in costumes appropriate to Christmas. Dress the tallest child in a red Santa costume and the chorus in green or white. If green is used, a minstrel-type hood and shoes could be added. White dresses with red or green headbands and mittens would give a pleasing effect.

The pantomime should be explained to the audience in advance. This can be done by a narrator, or the outline given here can be printed on your program.

a) Christmas Tree. (1) Tramp through the forest to find the tree. (March, lifting knees high, as if walking in deep snow.) (2) Chop it down. Children in a circle, each one with an ax, chopping. (Waltz music.) (3) Carry trees home on the shoulders. Each child puts his left hand on the shoulder of the one in front, and places his right hand at his own right shoulder, as if holding a branch. (4) Children face the center of the circle, advance, and place the tree in the center, then retreat to places.

b) Christmas Bells. Children standing in a circle, pull the bell

71

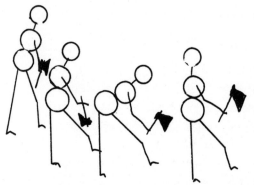

rope. (Waltz music.) March and and toll the bell.

c) Santa Claus. Children stand in a double line to represent reindeer. First two join hands; the outside hands are extended back to be grasped by the ones behind. Children on the left extend right hand forward and left hand back, and the children on the right, vice versa. One child is at the end of the long double line for "Santa Claus." "Reindeer walk" — step high and trot very gently, lifting the feet high and placing them lightly.

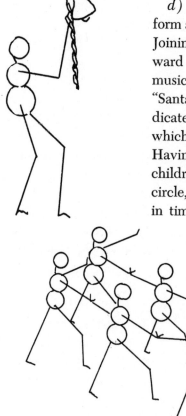

d) Christmas Toys. Children form a ring around "Santa Claus." Joining hands, they advance toward him four steps with the music, and back. As they do this, "Santa Claus," in the center, indicates the use of some toy which he pretends to give them. Having retreated to place, the children advance around the circle, imitating "Santa Claus," in time to the music.

1) Ball. Tossing up and catch-
   ing. (Waltz music.)
2) Skates. Long sliding steps, as
   if on the ice. (Two-step music.)
3) Drum. (Beating.)
4) Hoop. (Waltz music.) Run
   lightly, striking hoop in time
   with the music.

Madrigals and Carols

Six or eight people with good natural voices can add a rare touch to the program by singing some English madrigals. They should wear sixteenth- or seventeenth-century costumes and sit around a long candle-lighted table. Madrigals are sung without accompaniment. Some of the old carols can be found in arrangements suitable for a madrigal group, or they can be sung with the familiar harmonized settings.

Madrigals are polyphonic, that is, they are composed of several melodies, no one being more important than another. Charles Kennedy Scott dates the heyday of the English madrigal from 1588 to 1698 in his *Madrigal Singing* (London, Oxford University Press, 1931). This book is both a history and a textbook, with valuable appendices giving a list of madrigals, ballets, and ayres (the two latter are related types of choral music) published during the Elizabethan period.

The Oxford University Press has also published a selection of madrigals under the title *Euterpe*. These can be bought separately.

Most of the madrigals are love songs or pastorals. Some composers set portions from the psalms in madrigal style, and these would be appropriate for a Christmas program.

14. CHRISTMAS ENTERTAINMENT IN CHURCHES, SCHOOLS, AND COMMUNITY CENTERS

Blowing in the Yule

A medieval European city on the North Sea had a beautiful custom, observed for hundreds of years, which was called "blowing in the yule." On Christmas Eve, near midnight, four trumpeters mounted to a high tower which dominated the town. The tower had four sides, and each trumpeter took his place at one of them. Then, toward the four corners of the earth — north, east, south, and west — they trumpeted Christmas carols and hymns. The first hymn played was always Martin Luther's "A Mighty Fortress Is Our God." This ceremony is worthy of adoption in any community where there is a tower or high place.

Moravian Trombone Welcome

On Christmas morning, the Moravian Trombone Choir takes its place in the tower of the old Moravian Church in Bethlehem, Pennsylvania, and plays "How Brightly Shines the Morning Star." More recently, the star that lights the way to the city has been a hundred-foot-high electric fixture erected on top of South Mountain. The choir tours the principal streets, singing glad tidings — "Peace on earth, good will to men" — and the trombones give a ringing note to the message.

Plundering the Christmas Tree

With everything stepped up, as it is in our present-day world, many families have to end their holiday festivities on New Year's Day, instead of waiting until Twelfth-night. In this case, celebrate New Year's Eve on New Year's Day by ceremoniously taking down the greens.

In some Scandinavian countries they call this a "plundering party." For families living in small communities, it makes a happy ending of holiday gaieties, for the children will accept the early dismantling of the Christmas tree with greater fortitude if it is made a jolly occasion.

In the countries where this custom originated, groups of people meet at the village square and go from house to house to "plunder" the Christmas trees. In larger communities over here, a number of families might get together and plan their party according to their number and their household facilities.

In each home the hostess and the children dismantle the tree in advance and place the ornaments on a tray. Simple refreshments — cookies, beverages, etc. — are spread out on a table. Each guest is allowed to select a tree ornament to take home with him.

When all the homes have been visited, the bare trees are carried out to the village square or an appropriate spot to be burned. As the huge bonfire flares up, all the company sing the Christmas carols for the last time, this season, and then sing a New Year's carol and "Auld Lang Syne" as the bells ring at midnight.

The following Christmas, the bells and stars will adorn trees in new homes. The young people will remember incidents of various plundering parties and will recall the former owners of the ornaments as they hang them on their own trees.

Prologue for a Christmas Party

The party which the church provides for the children during the holidays will be more enjoyable as well as more manageable if there is a prepared introduction to set the mood for the rest of the entertainment.

Hang a large holly wreath in the center of the stage or platform. If the auditorium is all level, hang the wreath between the windows at one end and have the piano at one side. Have two large floor candelabra to the right and left of the wreath, with red candles. When the children have assembled, two of the older ones, previously selected and wearing costumes, light the candles. Two others — a boy and a girl — act as readers. When the candles have been lighted, the first reader comes forward.

Reader: It's Christmas! Holly wreaths and mistletoe, evergreens and brightly lighted candles! Fireworks in the south, sleigh bells in the north, all say "Merry Christmas." And as we light these candles, we think of Him whose birthday we celebrate.

All sing: "Deck the halls, with boughs of holly . . . " an old Welsh air.

Second reader: The custom of singing from door to door, "wassailing," as they called it, was and still is a popular Christmas custom. Waifs went about the streets carrying lanterns, singing and receiving small change and bits of pastry for their songs.

All sing: "Here we come a-wassailing . . . " a traditional English carol.

(A small band of waifs might sing the verses, with the company joining in the chorus.)

First reader: Today the Christmas carols tell of the birth of the Christ child in familiar and beautiful songs, and most of them bear the message of that Christmas long ago when light came into the world.

(The room is darkened and all sing "Silent Night.")

Second reader: May the spirit of the Christmas story enter all our hearts and help us to carry with us love and good will wherever we go until Christmas comes again.

All sing: "God rest you merry, gentlemen . . ." traditional English carol.

Then the rest of your program can follow.

— *By* OLEDA SCHROTTHY

Carve an Angel from Candle

Buy a plain white candle and carve your own Christmas figures. Mark the design on the candle and gradually carve away the wax with a knife or carving tools. Add color with oil paints.

CHRISTMAS PAGEANTS

Naming the Baby

Here is a Christmas theme so simple in its conception that it can be produced in a church, a school, or even in a house, and with very little rehearsal. The cast may have any number of individuals, whose ages may vary from the very old to the very young.

The pageant has two acts. The first depicts a long procession of people traveling along a highway to Bethlehem to pay their taxes. The second is a tableaux-like scene of a stable, showing the Holy Family surrounded by the travelers who have come to admire the baby. All participants are dressed in loosely-draped costumes similar to those worn in Biblical times. While the dialogue is largely ad libbed, some preparation should be made so one or two trained leaders can play the principal roles, thereby assuring the play's continuity.

The highway can be in front of the closed stage curtain if it is set back far enough to allow the people to walk between it and the footlights. To make it more realistic, cut trees and shrubbery out of green and brown paper and fasten them on the curtain. In the center is a small house or booth where all must stop and pay their taxes. Divide all the participants into small families; this gives a natural grouping for all ages, even babies, if anyone wishes to carry one.

As each family stops to pay taxes, the collector asks about different members of the family —— how they have prospered during the year — or observes how tall the children have grown, etc.

79

Since this person must do most of the talking, it is important to select someone who speaks well, has plenty of repartee and good taste. The conversation can take many turns, depending on the amount of time available for preparation and the number of people that must pass by the booth.

The second act takes place on the main part of the stage, where all the people who were in the procession are gathered to form a tableaux as the curtain rises. Joseph and Mary are on either side of the crib or manger, and if you want, you may have the Wise Men and shepherds as they are usually placed in a Nativity scene. The group can be singing carols or Christmas music may be heard in the distance.

Now comes the main feature of the second act — "What to name the Baby?" Here you must go to the library to find the significant boys' names, or you will be able to find some given in the Bible. The most ancient methods of name giving were to choose on the basis of some event taking place at birth or some quality desired in the child. If no inspiration occurred, the child was later named for some striking characteristic or early action.

Let different members of the cast step forward with a suggested name and prepare a few lines to signify its meaning. The climax comes when a familiar carol, "Away in a manger, no crib for a bed, the little Lord Jesus laid down his sweet head . . ." is heard in the distance and Mary says, "The baby shall be called 'Jesus.'"

We have made a list of Hebrew names with their meanings; if you want to find others, consult *Dictionary of Given Names*, by Florence Haines Longhead (The Arthur H. Clark Co., Glendale 4, California).

Abraham — first of the patriarchs and father of the Hebrew nation.

Adam — oldest known name — "made in the image of God."

Amariah — "whom God has promised."

Amos — "borne by God" — honoring herdsmen of Bethlehem.

Asa — "a healer," "a physician"— in the Bible, King of Judah.

Aza — "the noble" — noble name.

David — "beloved" — shepherd who became King of Israel.

Isaac — "laughter" — born to Abraham and Sarah when she was old. Sarah cried in her joy. "God has made me laugh."

Jesus — "the healer."

Joseph — "he shall add" — gave name to firstborn so others would follow.

Joshua — "Jehovah is deliverance" — successor of Moses.

Judah — "the praised" — one of the world's greatest leaders.

Michael — "who is like God."

Moses — "a great leader or lawgiver."

Nathaniel — "gift of God."

Noah — "rest, comfort."

Reuben — "behold a son" — said by Leah.

Sabian — "host of heavens, wisdom of the gods is he."

Samuel — "asked of God," "name of God," "heard of God."

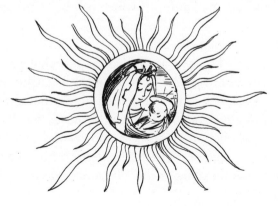

Christmas Everywhere

A Short Pageant for Clubs

Preparations for the celebration may be simple or elaborate, according to resources and time. Use ingenuity for costumes and in making properties. If there is no Christmas tree to be had, find a hoop or a piece of wire which can be made into a hoop. Cover it with cloth, greens, or if there is paint at hand, just color it. Tie to the hoop popcorn balls, bags of candy, fruit, or little packages, and suspend the hoop from the ceiling. This is the Christmas crown described in another part of this book (See page 50). In Sweden, where the crown originated, they often have candle holders with lighted candles fastened to the top of the crown. Such details will depend on the time and place where your Christmas party is to be held.

The speaking parts of the following play may be read. The principal characters who carry the continuity of the festival might get together for half an hour of rehearsal beforehand. The characters are:

| First Reader | Ten persons for Nativity scene |
| Second Reader | Chorus: All in attendance |

The festival opens with a processional, including either the entire attendance or those who are the special participants, singing, "O Come, All Ye Faithful," which can be found in any hymn book.

When all are in place —

First Reader: Christmas again. No matter what happens in between, Christmas always comes — the most beautiful season of the whole year. Each one of us is absorbed in the thought of this holy time, as one understands it. To many it means family gatherings, brisk walks, packages, the smell of baking cookies, Christmas trees, a dance, turkey or goose, our favorite dessert. But, more than that, it is the spiritual meaning of the Christmas season that is deep in our hearts.

COSTUMES

Once, long ago, Phillips Brooks, that great preacher, spent Christmas in the Holy Land, and looking out upon Bethlehem on Christmas Eve, he eased his heart by writing that hymn we all know so well.

> (*Here follows, sung by the assembly, "O Little Town of Bethlehem," found in any hymnal. Here, if it is appropriate and possible in your location, a Nativity scene may follow. Mary is seated at the manger. Joseph stands beside her. A light from the manger shines on her face. An angel stands in the background.*)

Second Reader: "And there were in the same country shepherds abiding in the field; keeping watch over their flocks by night. And, lo, the angel of the Lord came upon them and the glory of the Lord shone round about them: and they were sore afraid. And the Angel said unto them: "Fear not: for, behold, I bring you good tidings of great joy, which shall be to all people. For unto you is born this day in the City of David a Saviour, which is Christ the Lord."

> (*If it seems better to omit the Nativity scene, let the First Reader read Isaiah 42: 1-9, and then let the Second Reader read St. Luke 2: 7-14.*)

All in attendance sing "The First Noel," found in many hymnals and song collections.

> (*While the carol is being sung, shepherds come from left and kneel at manger.*)

First Reader: As Christmas was celebrated through the years, it lost a great deal of its Christian meaning, and often became nothing more than a celebration devoid of spiritual significance. King Alfred in the year 878 held such high Christmas revelry that he was attacked by the Danes, taken quite unaware, and his army annihilated. In 1621 in Puritan New England, Governor Bradford rebuked certain lusty men because they refused to work on Christmas Day, and in 1643 the Roundhead Parliament abolished the observance of holy days and saints' days altogether. But Christmas could not be ruled out. It is a birthday we all rejoice to keep. So

84

let us make merry and, as the old rhyme goes —

> "Without the door let sorrow lie
> And if for cold it hap' to die,
> We'll bury it in a Christmas pye
> And evermore be merry."

Second Reader: In America, on Christmas Eve, there is a Santa Claus who fills children's stockings with toys and leaves the gifts too large for stockings beneath an evergreen tree which is covered with bright ornaments.

Good Saint Nicholas, the ancestor of Santa Claus, visits the children in many countries in Europe, where he is recognized and loved.

In Lapland they have a Christmas goat, called Old Man Christmas. He wears a hooded fur coat, long whiskers, and a false nose, and is not a goat at all — that is just an affectionate term — but a benefactor like our Santa Claus.

From England comes the good old custom of bringing in the yule log.

(Here follows a yule log procession while the assembly sings "Come Bring with a Noise," found in the New Beacon Octavo, No. 607, Silver Burdett Company, 43 East 17 Street, New York, N. Y. If this is not possible, have a candle-lighting ceremony, the Reader speaking as follows while the candles are being lighted:)

First Reader:

> "Some sayes, that ever 'gainst that Season comes
> Wherein our Saviour's Birth is celebrated,
> The Bird of Dawning singeth all night long;
> And then (they say) no Spirit can walke abroad,
> The nights are wholesome, then no Planets strike,
> No Faery talkes, nor Witch hath power to Charme:
> So halloed, and so gracious is the time."

SHAKESPEARE

No Christmas party is complete without the mummers or "geese dancers," as they are sometimes called. The custom of masking, or "mumming," was popular both in eastern and western Europe. The mummers claimed the right to enter any place. Sometimes they danced and sang, but frequently they presented a play. The customary drama had to do with the adventures of Saint George and the Dragon, and the bringing back of the slain to life by the doctor. Sometimes the mummers did the morris dances and the sword dances so popular in England. Perhaps everyone in our gathering might like to join in the dancing led by the mummers.

(The dance might be any circle dance, a grand right and left, perhaps until the leader calls, "Choose a partner." Then all find a partner and dance. After ten or fifteen minutes, if the dancing is going well, — sooner if it seems desirable, — jugglers, magicians, and anyone who can entertain the party appear. If the leader knows of talent within the group assembled, he can round them up while the dancing is going on. Everyone is seated while the artists perform their tricks. After each has done his bit, carol singers enter carrying a wassail bowl. It is put down on the table and all sing "God Rest Ye Merry, Gentlemen." Sleigh bells are heard, followed by stamping and tramping. Enter Santa Claus. He calls out, "Merry Christmas. Christmas, Christmas, Everywhere." He is carrying a Christmas tree and he asks two of the audience to go out for his pack.)

Santa Claus: Come light the candles — gather round the bowl — let's make merry. Here is a tree to be trimmed — come, all.

(Here follows a party — some string popcorn and hang it on the tree, others fasten bits of paper, tin, and cardboard to the bough. Others fasten candles or lights. Everyone drinks Christmas punch, eats cookies, popcorn balls, etc. When the tree is trimmed and the candles are lighted and the party has toned down, all sing "Silent Night." Before Santa leaves, he empties his pack and exits calling "Merry Christmas to all and to all a good night." All shout, "Merry Christmas.")

Raising the Star

A beautiful custom called "raising the star," sometimes referred to as "hanging the greens," takes place in St. George's Church in New York City each year a few days before Christmas. Here parishioners, as in the English village churches, come to prepare their church for the day of Nativity. While the choir sings Christmas songs to the deep notes of the organ, willing workers are weaving great panels of laurel and rhododendron to bring greenery into the church for the holiday festivities.

The greens are woven into panels which were constructed especially for this purpose and always kept from year to year. Each one is a wooden frame, approximately 3 feet by 6 feet, with chicken wire in the center, as shown in the drawing. They are painted green to correspond with the foliage and are placed at the ends of the pews. The people stand as they work. Just before the festivities begin, piles of fresh  laurel or rhododendron sprays are placed in the center of each one, the stems of which are to be woven in and out of the holes in the wire mesh. A special group of men are on the balcony, weaving garlands which are later hung in loops around the choir loft, and little children go to the pulpit to take part in decorating a life-size crèche to be used later as a tableau.

The festivities begin with everyone extending Christmas greetings and welcoming newcomers to the church. One of the elders acts as host and invites everyone to take part in decorating the church. He also explains how to weave the greens so the finished panels will be completely covered. As busy fingers are twining laurel twigs into the wire panel, the choir sings familiar Christmas carols; the weavers may join in, or they may converse with their neighbors — whichever they choose. When all panels are completed, they are placed around the walls of the church, but enough are reserved to make a solid screen across the front of the pulpit and the children's crèche. The garlands are draped around the choir loft and the balcony, so the church is literally covered with beautiful waxy greens. The congregation is asked to be seated, and when all is quiet, the lights are turned out for a moment and the Christmas pageant begins.

A spotlight is turned on the minister, who reads the Christmas story. The organist begins to play, ever so softly, and a dim light appears above the panels in front of the pulpit. As the music becomes stronger, a star begins to rise from behind the greens, and it ascends slowly in the darkened church. Borne aloft on strands of laurel rope, the star shines high over the crèche below. The choir and congregation alike rise and sing out full-voiced, and the lights in the church burn brightly again. With a throb in their throats, the workers, their job completed, watch the shining star that once rose over the little town of Bethlehem, and kneel for the benediction. Then finding tongue anew, they call, "Merry Christmas," to their friends and neighbors and the strangers within their gates.

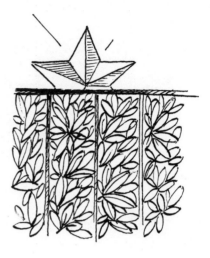

15. AN OLD ENGLISH CHRISTMAS

The phrase "an Old English Christmas" is familiar to every American, but very few know the significance of all the characters and the sequence of their appearance. We have endeavored to piece together the customs and entertainment as they actually took place in the early centuries in England so that readers can adapt them to pageants, pantomimes, and even parties.

Here, in a few words, is a description of an Old English Christmas, details of which are given on the following pages.

The lord of the manor invited the people from the countryside to a Christmas celebration at the castle. They assembled in the great dining room to partake of a Christmas feast. After the guests were seated, a boar's head was carried in during the singing of the "Boar's Head Carol."

When the feast was over, the guests assembled in the drawing room for the entertainment that followed. This included the following events in the order listed:

1) Lighting of the yule log by the lord of the castle.
2) Admitting a weary Traveler who told stories from many lands.
3) Weary Traveler's removing ragged clothes and becoming the Lord of Misrule. He is master of ceremonies for the celebration, and the fun begins.

4) Sword dance.
   Morris dance.
5) Mummers give play — always about Saint George and the Dragon.
6) Singing by the carolers.
7) Pantomime of Mother Goose by children.
8) Group dance, "Sweet Kate."

One can easily plan a Christmas festival, pantomime, or even a party by following this outline. The theme can be carried out by adapting the material to the talent and space at hand. For instance, the feast may be omitted, or the yule log ceremony, if you have no fireplace, etc. If the party is carefully planned, it may be used over and over, since the theme is traditional with the American people.

The following poem might be an appropriate opening for the party:

> Welcome Yule, thou merry man,
> In worship of this holy day!
>
> Welcome be Thou, Heavenly King,
> Welcome, born in one morning,
> Welcome, for Whom we shall sing,
>
> Welcome, Yule. . . .
>
> Welcome be ye, Stephen and John,
> Welcome, Innocents, every one,
> Welcome Thomas, Martyr one,
>
> Welcome, Yule. . . .
>
> Welcome be ye that are here,
> Welcome all, and make good cheer,
> Welcome all another year,
>
> Welcome, Yule. . . .

Now come the activities in the order they are given:

The Boar's Head

Although there are some modern imitations of this rite, many of us feel that there is a touch of grossness about it. However, in Medieval England the boar was an enemy to be reckoned with. Travel then was chiefly afoot, and there were thick forests and long, lonely stretches to be traversed where the wayfarer might have to encounter one or more of them. Therefore, the boar's head, borne in procession to the table of my lord and lady in the great hall, signified a victory over evil.

The "Boar's Head Carol" is a secular song which was composed to accompany this rite, and is found at the back of this book (*See* page 173). This carol was sung in procession, with many local variations. One can imagine travelers from one part of England to another relating how extraordinary the procession was in *their* districts the year before. A trumpeter announced the boar's head; then came a line of pages, heralds, torchbearers, trumpeter, and two minstrels carrying the trophy, which was placed before the host at the head of the table, while guests and servants joined in the singing.

The Traveler

Hospitality was a sacred obliga-
tion in the olden days, especially
at Christmastime. And so to every
feast there came a symbolic character — the Traveler, a cold and
hungry wanderer. He knocked on
the door, and when it was opened

by one of the servants, he begged for food and warmth, promising
to entertain the company with the story of his adventures. He was
welcomed and taken to the hearth, where he told his tale. Then
he took off his ragged costume and revealed that he was none other
than the Lord of Misrule, come to make their Christmas jolly. He
called in his companions, the mummers and jesters, and the fun
began.

The Lord of Misrule

The traditional master of revelry used to be chosen on Hal-
loween, which shows how important the ancient Christmas celebrations were, since the people began to think of them as far back
as October. As we recalled in the introduction, (See page 1),
Christmastide used to last until Candlemas Day, which falls on
February 2. The Lord of Misrule was therefore a very important
person, indeed, for he had to keep things lively and merry for forty

days. Cakes and ale were the special reward to him and his com-
rades, and of course they shared
all the host's bounty.

The Yule Log Procession

While all present sang a gay
song, the pages brought in the
yule log and placed it on the
hearth. The yule sprite (the

93

youngest member of the assembly) rode astride the log. The head of the house touched it off with a brand from last year's log, and as the flame mounted high, the guests drank toasts and shouted greetings, for it was believed that a blazing yule log would bring good fortune during the coming year. As the log crackled and burned, someone would start up another song, for those were singing Christmases. See pages 65-66 for yule log ceremonies.

Hoodman-Blind

A boisterous part of the fun began when the Lord of Misrule and his followers placed a hood over the head of one of the guests, and started the rough and tumble Old English game of hoodman-blind, popular during the fifteenth and sixteenth centuries. This was how our American game of blindman's buff originated.

The Waits

By this time the waits would have arrived, singing their way from door to door.

Originally the "waits" were minstrels of the king's court, whose duty it was to watch and call the hours. But by the sixteenth century the word had come to mean a band of people who went from house to house singing Christmas carols. A favorite old song of theirs was "Here we come a-wassailing," which you will find on page 178.

The Wassail Bowl

After the main portion of the feast was over, the wassail was brought. Many spontaneous songs had their inspiration in this ceremony. The bowl contained the choicest ale, flavored with spices and sugar, with roasted apples floating in it. (It is now often made from sweet cider.) Cups were filled from the steaming bowl and each guest drank his neighbor's health. The word *"wassail"* comes from the Old English greeting, *wes hal,* or *waes hael,* which means "Be thou whole," or as we would say, "To your health," or "Good luck."

The Mummers

The mummers came in with the Lord of Misrule and presented their famous play. It was a combination of gay nonsense and mock heroics.

Although the dialogue varied from year to year, the plot and the characters of the mummers' play were always the same: it told of the slaying of the Dragon and the Giant Turpin by Saint George, the patron of England. (*See* Reginald J. Tiddy, *The Mummers' Play* [London and New York: The Claredon Press, 1923], or use the play on pages 103-106.)

The Morris Dance

The Morris Men, with their tinkling bells and painted sticks, danced for the assembly.

You will find some of their dances described in Elizabeth Burchenal, *Folk Dances From Old Homeland.* (New York, G. Schirmer, Inc., 1922) and Cecil Sharp, *The Morris Book,* Vol I (London, Novello and Co., Ltd., 1912). Your public library will probably have other books containing the music and steps of these picturesque old dances.

The Mother Goose Pantomime

Mother Goose made an annual appearance at Christmas time. No one knows just how her name originated, but it is supposed to be from Queen Goosefoot of French legend, who dearly loved children. The rhymes were passed from parent to child by word of mouth long years before they appeared in print. That was about 1760, and since then they have been foremost among the children's favorites, not only in England and America, but on the continent of Europe as well. An outline of a typical Mother Goose pantomime can be found on pages 98-101.

The Sword Dance

The sword was a mark of rank and authority (it still is, for that matter). It was the young nobles from the countryside who unsheathed their swords and did the English sword dance, finally weaving all their swords into a star.

The sword dance, the morris dance, and the mummers' play all grew out of the old mystery play.

Cecil Sharp's *Sword Dances of Northern England*, Vol. I (London, Novello and Co., Ltd., 1912), can be found in some reference libraries, and your local library will help you find other descriptions of this dance.

The Country Dance

Then came the time for everybody to dance. The lord and lady of the house probably sat in the observers' seats as the country lads and lasses found their partners and took to the floor. The most popular of all dances in England during the sixteenth century was "Sweet Kate." You will find the music and steps described on pages 107-108.

Carols

The festivities ended with carol singing by everybody before they made ready to go to the parish church (or it might have been to an abbey church or a cathedral) for the midnight service. Words and tunes of several of the much-loved old carols are given later on, and the following books are recommended for those who wish to delve deeper into this rich mine of English song: *The Oxford Book of Carols*. Comp. and ed. by Pery Dearmer, R. Vaughan Williams, and Martin Shaw (London, Oxford University Press, 1928).

Christmas Carols, New and Old. The words edited by the Rev. Henry Ransden Bramley. The music edited by Sir John Stainer. (London, Novello and Co., Ltd.)

This delightful Christmas entertainment can include all the children in the group, and it can be given with very little preparation and rehearsal.

Mother Goose should be one of the older girls. She wears a pointed black hat and a long black cape over a bright red skirt.

She is the only character who has any lines to speak. They need not be memorized, for she can have a little book as one of her properties (or it might be a large Mother Goose book) and part of her business can be to consult it. The book will also contain a list of the rhymes to be pantomimed, in their order. She should know the rhymes by heart, but she can look in the book to prompt herself on their sequence without seeming to depend upon it.

Some of the scenes will require several characters and some, only one. Arrange them so that the solo parts come in-between the group scenes.

There should be a background of appropriate music such as Humperdinck's score for *Hansel and Gretel*, etc.

Properties and Stage Setting

The properties will depend upon the rhymes selected. A small table and several chairs will certainly be needed. If given on a dais or a stage, there should be a curtain, screens, or some other sort of backdrop. Pine branches, potted trees, and large potted plants will make an attractive background. Large candelabra on either side or tall candlesticks with lighted candles on two tables upstage would be effective, standing before the greens of the drop.

Place the properties behind the curtain at one side of the stage and have a "property man" in charge.

If you have Jack Horner, have a hassock for him to sit on. Miss Muffet should have a small bench. The spider can be made from black stockings, with wire legs wound with narrow black-fringed crepe paper sewed to the stuffed body and white buttons for eyes. A concealed stagehand can operate the spider by a string, and so on with all the other appurtenances.

The Costumes

If you want other authentic costumes, consult *The Real Mother Goose*, by M. Winter, (New York, Rand, McNally Co.) or get any well-illustrated Mother Goose book and follow it. Bright-colored paper, cambric, crepe paper, figured materials, and Canton flannel can be used. The medieval style should at least be suggested, according to tradition. For a hasty performance, improvise effects from whatever is at hand.

The Pantomime

This is only a suggestion of how you might do the pantomime. You will have many thoughts of your own. If it is going to be impromptu, the director should have a clear idea of the interpretation of the rhymes, and at least two good assistants, perhaps from among the older children. Have a quick rehearsal of each sketch.

(*Mother Goose enters, perturbed. She is turning over the pages of a large red book.*)

Mother Goose: Well, well, it will be wonderful to have all the children together again. But confusing, too, with such a large family as mine. . . . I think I'll see them one at a time, and then let them all have a romp in the hall. (*Looks off-stage.*) There's Tommy Green. . . . Always up to tricks, putting pussy in the well, or something mischievous. I'll give him something to do. . . . That will keep him out of trouble for a while. Tommy, Tommy. . . .

(*Enter Tommy, with a shamefaced look.*)

Mother Goose: Tommy, I want to see the rest of the family one at a time, so you be a good boy, and stay here and bring them to me.

(Tommy bobs his head, not quite daring to look Mother Goose in the eye.)

Mother Goose: Mistress Mary, if you please, Tommy.

(Tommy goes off-stage and brings back Mistress Mary, accompanied by four little girls (her flowers), who squat down in a row, facing audience, while Mistress Mary goes down the line with her watering can. As she sprinkles each one, it revives and stands up straight and smiling.)

Mother Goose: Mistress Mary, quite contrary,
How does your garden grow?
With silver bells, and cockleshells,
And pretty maids all in a row.

(As she finishes, they all turn to her, make a curtsy, and exit, ushered by Tommy Green.)

Mother Goose: Jack Sprat and his wife.

(While Tommy brings them in, Mother Goose moves the little table to the center and places a chair on each side. Jack and his wife each bring a platter and a fork. They seat themselves and eat busily, making a great clatter with their forks as Mother Goose recites their rhyme.)

Mother Goose: Jack Sprat could eat no fat,
His wife could eat no lean,
And so between the two of them
They licked the platter clean.

(They rise, bow to Mother Goose, and are led out by Tommy Green.)

Mother Goose: (*reading from book*)

> Christmas is acoming,
> The geese are getting fat,
> Please put a penny in the old man's hat.
> > If you haven't got a penny,
> A ha'penny will do,
> If you haven't got a ha'penny,
> > God bless you!

(*While she has been reciting this slowly, the old man has come in, helped by Tommy, and has been standing hat in hand, while children have been filing by dropping pennies into his hat. One child goes slowly by with a large purse which he shakes upside down to show that it is empty, and the old man raises his hand in blessing and shakes his head over this penniless one.*)

And so on, with Little Jack Horner, the Queen and Knave of Hearts, Little Miss Muffet, and all the others.

As a grand finale, they all return to the stage, surround Mother Goose, who walks about among them, patting and hugging them, and then all join in singing one of the rhymes to a familiar tune, as, for instance, "Bye-o Baby Bunting."

101

The Mummers' Play

The mummers' play always dealt with only one subject — Saint George and the Dragon. One version of it is given on pages 103-106 of this chapter. There are three books, all out of print but often available in large libraries, which give a number of authentic versions of the play. They are Peter H. Ditchfield, *Old English Customs* (London, Methuen & Co., 1901); Thselton F. Dyer, *British Popular Customs* (London, G. Bell and Sons, Ltd., 1888); and Thomas K. Hervey, *The Book of Christmas* (London, Roberts Bros., 1888).

The mummers always marched around the hall before they began, clowning, smirking, and strutting. They bowed deeply to my lord and lady before beginning the play, and at the end they passed their hats around the banquet table.

The Christmas Play of Saint George and the Dragon
From a Lost Medieval Miracle Play

CHARACTERS

Saint George Father Christmas King of Egypt The Giant Turpin
The Dragon   The Doctor   Turkish Knight

(Enter the Turkish Knight.)

Turkish Knight: Open your doors, and let me in,
                   I hope your favors I shall win;
                   Whether I rise or whether I fall,
                   I'll do my best to please you all.
                   St. George is here, and swears he will come in,
                   And, if he does, I know he'll pierce my skin.
                   If you will not believe what I do say,
                   Let Father Christmas come in — clear the way.
                         (Retires.)

(Enter Father Christmas.)

Father Christmas: Here come I, old Father Christmas,
                     Welcome, or welcome not,
                 I hope old Father Christmas
                   Will never be forgot.
                 I am not come here to laugh or to jeer,
                   But for a pocketful of money, and a skinful
                     of beer,
                 If you will not believe what I do say,
                 Come in the King of Egypt — clear the way.

(Enter the King of Egypt.)

King of Egypt: Here I, the King of Egypt, boldly do appear,
               Saint George, Saint George, walk in, my only son
                   and heir.
               Walk in, my son Saint George, and boldly act thy
                   part,
               That all the people here may see thy wond'rous
                   art.

(Enter Saint George.)

Saint George: Here come I, Saint George, from Britain did I
>> spring,
>> I'll fight the Dragon bold, my wonders to begin.
>> I'll clip his wings, he shall not fly;
>> I'll cut him down, or else I die.

(Enter the Dragon.)

Dragon: Who's he that seeks the Dragon's blood,
>> And calls so angry, and so loud?
>> That English dog, will he before me stand?
>> I'll cut him down with my courageous hand.
>> With my long teeth, and scurvy jaw,
>> Of such I'd break up half a score,
>> And stay my stomach, till I'd more.

(Saint George and the Dragon fight, the latter is killed.)

Father Christmas: Is there a doctor to be found
>> All ready, near at hand,
>> To cure a deep and deadly wound,
>> And make the champion stand.

(Enter Doctor.)

Doctor: Oh! yes, there is a doctor to be found
>> All ready, near at hand,
>> To cure a deep and deadly wound,
>> And make the champion stand.

Father Christmas: What can you cure?

Doctor: All sorts of diseases,
>> Whatever you pleases,
>> The phthisic, the palsy, and the gout;
>> If the devil's in, I'll blow him out.

Father Christmas: What is your fee?

Doctor: Fifteen pound, it is my fee,
>> The money to lay down.
>> But, as 'tis such a rogue as thee,
>> I cure for ten pound.

I carry a little bottle of alicumpane;
    Here Jack, take a little of my flip flop,
    Pour it down thy tip top;
Rise up and fight again.

(The Doctor performs his cure, the fight is renewed,
and the Dragon again killed.)

Saint George: Here am I, Saint George,
    That worthy champion bold,
    And with my sword and spear
    I won three crowns of gold.
    I fought the fiery dragon,
        And brought him to the slaughter;
    By that I won fair Sabra,
        The King of Egypt's daughter.
    Where is the man, that now will me defy?
    I'll cut his giblets full of holes, and make his but-
                tons fly.

(The Turkish Knight advances.)

Turkish Knight: Here come I, the Turkish Knight,
    Come from the Turkish land to fight.
    I'll fight Saint George, who is my foe,
    I'll make him yield before I go;
    He brags to such a high degree,
    He thinks there's none can do the like of he.

Saint George: Where is the Turk, that will before me stand?
    I'll cut him down with my courageous hand.

(They fight, the Kinght is overcome and falls on one knee.)

Turkish Knight: Oh! pardon me, Saint George, pardon of thee I
        crave,
        Oh! pardon me this night, and I will be thy
        slave.

Saint George: No pardon shalt thou have, while I have foot to
        stand.
        So rise thee up again, and fight out sword in hand.

(They fight again, and the Knight is killed. Father Christmas calls for the Doctor, the same dialogue occurs as before.)

(Enter Giant Turpin.)

Giant Turpin: Here come I, the Giant, bold Turpin is my name,
　　　　　And all the nations round do tremble at my fame.
　　　　　Wher'ere I go, they tremble at my sight,
　　　　　No lord or champion long with me would fight.

Saint George: Here's one that dares to look thee in the face,
　　　　　And soon will send thee to another place.

(They fight and the Giant is killed; medical aid is called in as before, and the cure is performed by the Doctor, to whom then is given a basin of girdy grout and a kick and driven out.)

Father Christmas: Now ladies and gentlemen, your sport is most ended,
　　　　　So prepare for the hat, which is highly commended.
　　　　　That hat it would speak, if it had but a tongue;
　　　　　Come throw in your money and think it no wrong.

106

Sweet Kate

The directions for this dance, as here presented, are, so far as is known, the oldest printed in a book. They appeared in *The English Dancing Master,* published in 1650. The book is now in the British Museum. The dance was well over a hundred years old when first published. You will find the music and dance pattern in the books by Cecil Sharp and Elizabeth Burchenal, already mentioned on page 95. It can also be found in Volume IV of *Gymnastic and Folk Dances,* by Mary Wood Hinman (New York, A. S. Barnes and Company, 1914-30). RCA Victor record #20444 gives the music.

There are two versions of the music and the steps: the original and a slightly fuller and more modern set of directions.

SWEET KATE

How to Dance "Sweet Kate" (taken from original source).

Longways for as many as will. Stand as in Virginia Reel.

Part I. *Step one.* Partners join inside hands. Run forward four counts. Fall back to place, four counts. Repeat.

Step two. All spring on left foot. Strike right foot against right foot of partner. Spring on right foot. Strike left foot against left foot of partner. Hold for one count. Slap partner on right with right hand. Slap partner on left with left hand.

Step three. Wind fists one around the other. Hold right first finger up. Wind fists again, hold up left first finger.

Step four. All turn single. Repeat steps one, two, and three.

Part II. Partners side. That again. Repeat steps two, three, and four of Part I.

Part III. Partners hook right arms and turn. Partners hook left arms and turn. Repeat steps two, three, and four of Part I.

16. CHRISTMAS IN MEXICO

Our Mexican neighbors have some Christmas customs which are akin in spirit to those of medieval and Elizabethan England, combining joy and playfulness with religious sentiment. Chief among these is the fiesta, or series of fiestas, called *Posadas*, beginning on December 16 and continuing nightly until Christmas Eve.

The story goes that Mary and Joseph (Maria and José) were nine days on the road from Nazareth to Bethlehem, Mary riding a burro and Joseph walking at her side. *Las Posadas* are ceremonial commemorations of this long journey. (The word *posada* means "lodging place," "inn," or even "hotel.")

As with all folk customs, many local touches are given to them, but in the main the *Posadas* are the same all over Mexico. Friends gather in the patio of a house and form a procession each evening. Sometimes nine families join together. (The number nine has a religious significance, and special power is attributed to nine days' prayer.) In this case, each family has the *Posada* for one night.

At the head of the procession walk Mary and Joseph. Sometimes a boy and girl carry a platform on which are figures of the holy pilgrims, an angel walking before them. In the company following will be seen the Wise Men, the shepherds, cows, mules, camels, the child Jesus, and the star of Bethlehem. All carry lighted tapers and sing carols and litanies.

Joseph knocks at a door and begs lodging for Mary. Someone behind the door — the cruel innkeeper — replies that there is no room. For eight nights, each night at a different door, they knock and are refused entrance. For this reason, Mexican children often call the *Posadas*, "Knock, Knock." At the ninth door, the holy pilgrims are recognized and welcomed. Songs of welcome and sometimes prayers follow, if the participants are very devout. There is a manger, or *nacimiento*, set up in the favored house, but it remains empty until the ninth night, Christmas Eve. Then the Christ child is laid in the manger while bells ring, whistles blow, and fireworks are set off. Afterward, all repair to the church for the *Missa da Gallo*, or Mass of the Cock.

Every night, however, the pilgrims are invited into a home, and there is a gay party, with singing, dancing, and refreshments. But the ninth night is of course the gayest of all. It is a great honor to put the Christ child into the *nacimiento,* and a godfather and godmother are chosen for this rite. The manger occupies a place of honor until February 2, the day when the Christ child's presentation at the Temple is celebrated; then the godparents raise the figure of the infant from the *nacimiento,* and it is dressed carefully and placed on a tray decorated with flowers. Afterward the godparents often give a party for all who took part in their *Posadas.* So ends the Christmas season for that year. The Mexicans have really nine high days of Christmas, and they maintain the oldest tradition of keeping the great feast in mind until Candlemas Day.

The Piñata

This is the part of the *Posadas* the Mexican children like best of all. It is their special fun.

A *piñata* is a clay jug made especially to hold toys and favors. Each night of the nine ceremonial evenings, after the procession, the children play the *piñata* game. In the patio of the house, or whatever place will best hold them, hanging from a stable moor-

111

ing of some kind, are several *piñatas*. One is filled with water; another, with confetti; another, with gifts, sweets, and fruits. This is the good *piñata*.

The *piñatas* are gaily decorated; some look like clowns or very fat people; some have roses, stars, or beautiful symbols on them. The children form a circle around the *piñatas*, and put one of their number in the center with his eyes blindfolded. He is given a stick and is permitted three tries at breaking the *piñata*. Of course, he hopes to break the good one. The other children, meanwhile, sing and dance around in a circle. If the first child does not succeed in breaking the *piñata*, another child tries. Sometimes they are showered with water or confetti if the wrong *piñata* is broken. But when the good one breaks, they scramble for the favors and eat the sweets. This is a very happy time for the Mexican children, who look forward to it for months. It would not be Christmas for them without the *piñata*. This is the song they sing as they dance around, waiting for the great moment:

On Breaking the Piñata

On the night of *Posadas*
The *piñata* is the best;
The most prudish little girl
Bursts forth with joy.
Hit it, hit it, hit it,
Don't lose the aim that
Gives the distance.

AL QUEBRAR LA PINATA

Moderato

En las no - ches de po - sa - das la pi - ña - ta es

lo me - jor; la ni - ña más re - mil - ga - da

se al - bo - ro - ta con - ar - dor.

Allegro

Da - le, da - le, da - le, no pier - das el

ti - no que de la dis - tan - cia se pier - de el cami - no.

The following is the song of the pilgrims in the *Posadas* processions. It takes the form of a colloquy between Saint Joseph and the innkeeper.

LAS POSADAS

¿ Quién les da - po - sa - da a es - tos pe - re -
gri - nos, que vie - nen can - sa
dos de - an - dar los ca - mi - nos?
Por más que di - gá - is que ve - nís ren -
di - dos, no da - mos po - sa - da
a des - co - no - ci - dos.

(The two Spanish songs, "La Piñata," and "Las Posadas," with the music and the English translation, are printed by permission of the publishers, D. C. Heath and Company, from their publication: "El Mundo Español," Volume II, by Lilia Mary Casis, and Rebecca Shim Swithzer. Boston: 1942, pp. 354, 355, 580, and 581.)

Las Posadas

SAINT JOSEPH
Who will give lodging
to these pilgrims,
who are tired out
from traveling the highways?

INNKEEPER
However much you may say
that you are worn out
we do not give lodging
to strangers.

SAINT JOSEPH
In the name of heaven,
I beg of you lodging,
since my beloved wife
can travel no longer.

INNKEEPER
There is no lodging here,
keep on moving
I cannot open to you,
don't be stupid.

SAINT JOSEPH
Don't be inhuman
and have pity,
for the God of the Heavens
will reward you for it.

INNKEEPER
Now you may go away
and not bother me,
because if I get mad
I'm going to beat you.

SAINT JOSEPH
We come worn out
from Nazareth;
I am a carpenter
by the name of Joseph.

INNKEEPER
Your name doesn't concern me;
let me sleep,
since I have already told you
that we are not to open to you.

SAINT JOSEPH
Lodging, dear Innkeeper,
for only one night,
the Queen of the Heavens
begs of you.

INNKEEPER
Well then if she is a queen
who asks it,
how is it that at night
she goes so unattended?

SAINT JOSEPH
My wife is Mary,
the Queen of the Heavens;
mother she will be
of the Divine Word.

INNKEEPER
Is it you, Joseph,
and your wife Mary?
Enter Pilgrims;
I did not know you.

SAINT JOSEPH
Happy be this house
that gives us lodging;
may God always give you
your sacred happiness.

INNKEEPER
Lodging we give you
with much happiness;
enter, honest Joseph,
enter with Mary.

CHORUS (From without)
Enter saintly pilgrims;
receive this ovation,
not from this poor dwelling
but from my heart.

CHORUS (From within)
This night is (made) of happiness,
Of pleasure, and of rejoicing,
because we give lodging here to
the Mother of the Son of God.

115

A Carol for Christmas Eve

(Suggested for dramatization in costume.)
Listen, lordlings, unto me, a tale I will you tell;
Which, as on this night of glee, in David's town befell;
Joseph came from Nazareth, with Mary, that sweet maid;
Weary were they, nigh to death, and for a lodging pray'd.
   Sing high, sing low, sing high, sing low, sing to and fro.
   Go tell it out with speed;
   Cry out and shout all round about,
   That Christ is born, indeed.
In the inn they found no room, a scanty bed they made;
Soon a Babe from Mary's womb was in the manger laid;
Forth He came as light through glass; He came to save us all,
In the stable ox and ass before their Maker fall.
   Sing high, sing low, etc.
Shepherds lay afield that night, to keep the silly sheep;
Hosts of Angels in their sight came down from heaven's high steep
Tidings! tidings! unto you, to you a Child is born,
Fairer than the drops of dew, and brighter than the morn.
   Sing high, etc.
Onward then the Angels sped, the shepherds onward went,
God was in His manger bed, in worship low they bent.
In the morning, see they mind, my masters one and all,
At the altar Him to find who lay within the stall.
   Sing high, sing low, etc.

17. THE MANY MOODS OF AMERICAN CHRISTMAS

Christmas in America is a compound of Christmas seals and decorated wrappings, of cards being addressed and gifts acknowledged; to some, an hour's devotion in church, to many more, *The Christmas Carol* and a recording of Lionel Barrymore's Scrooge played at the family gathering. There are many faces to the genial saint who cares for American children, just as individual and different as the racial strains of the people. But whatever the differences, the great American heart always cries out, "Good will to men."

To start on the Atlantic seaboard, where our nation began, along the crunchy snow-packed streets of old Boston and other New England villages, bands of carolers, ringing hand bells, lift their voices on Christmas Eve. All traffic stops to let the singers pass.

Down in New York, which was once New Amsterdam, old Saint Mark's renews the holiday legend of good Saint Nicholas and his attendant, Black Peter, who comes to reward good children and reprove those not quite so good. A block away, the congregation of St. George's Church prepares their church for the day of Nativity — a custom described on pages 87-89.

There is another phase of New York holiday history that remains today unforgotten in this most populous of all American cities. People there remember Clement Moore, who wrote *The Night Before Christmas,* and they make annual pilgrimages to his quiet resting place on the cliffs above the Hudson in Trinity Cemetery. A long procession of people turn away from the bustle of Broadway on Christmas Eve, and with lanterns on their shoulders, they make their way to the grave of Moore and to that of the son of Charles Dickens, the author of the noted *Christmas Carol,* which are not far apart. And as carols sound over their quiet graves, radios all over the land are bringing these two bits of Christmas lore to old and young, each year.

It is fitting that the early celebrations in Virginia and generally through the South should see an annual repetition in reborn Williamsburg. There, as in Colonial days, the yule log is brought in and lit with ancient ceremony amid scenes that George Washington and Thomas Jefferson would find familiar. Residents of the ancient Virginia capital act as hosts to the tourist folk who have come for the holiday celebrations. They raise mugs of wassail and toast this climax of the passing year and greet the one to come. The wassail that is drunk in Williamsburg is made from the time-tested recipe of the town. In all the places where

Americans of today remember their English forebears, they toast the season with hot mulled punch. They, too, go wassailing.

The usual way of making this festive drink is simple, and here it is:

Hot Mulled Punch

To the wassail base, beer, ale, etc., add 12 fat cloves, perfect, one for each month of the year.

the rind of a lemon	2 tablespoons lump or
12 broken bits of whole cinnamon	loaf sugar, crushed

Into the liquid that has been poured into an enamel-lined kettle, place the cloves, the sugar, and the cinnamon. Then drop in the peel of the lemon, in a long, thin curl of rind. Let steep slowly over a simmering flame, never coming to a boil. Serve hot, poured into a mug over a sprig of fresh mint if possible. This is the traditional wassail consumed from Christmas Eve to Epiphany, January 6, the last of the twelve days of Christmas. Fruit cake is traditionally served with mulled punch, but on Epiphany there is a rich spiced cake with fruits and almonds known as Twelfth-night Cake.

In Philadelphia, which treasures among its ancient churches the Old Swedes Church, Gloria Dei, to be found in the oldest part of the city, there still cluster some of the customs of these folk who established settlements which they named for their Queen, Christiana. Among descendants of these Swedish settlers, the legend of Saint Lucia is recalled, and with her candle-lighted wreath of leaves, the white-gowned Lucia Bride offers coffee and saffron cakes to all callers. Over the mountains, Wisconsin and other areas where Scandinavians have settled, the customs of the homeland are preserved. Traditional dinners begin with smörgasbord, expand with the *lutefish,* and culminate with *grot,* that rich, sweet rice pudding with its single lucky almond.

Through the parishes of ancient New Orleans and the surrounding Louisiana, the French ancestry of these folk can be detected in the decorations of the churches and shrines by the roadsides and in the crèches that are found carefully erected even in the smallest homes. Christmas Day is a family day as it was back in France; one on which to be devout and to attend the Midnight Mass. Up the broad Mississippi, the German groups which thronged to the Missouri town of St. Louis in early Federal decades remember the customs of their homeland and center their celebration on the Christmas tree. This tradition of the decorated Christmas tree with dazzling lights is one that America has made its own in a spectacular fashion. True to the ways developed across the broad Atlantic and the spirit of doing things together as a community that was born from the perils of the colonist and nurtured by the needs of the pioneer, Christmas trees have blossomed out in hamlet, town, and city, from the great one on the lawn of the White House to the neighborhood trees of New York and other cities, as well as those of small villages over the whole country.

Down amid the sun-parched streets of New Mexican villages and in the pueblos, Americans whose ancestors came from Spain to the New World light little fires, which they call *"luminarias,"* before the front steps of their homes to guide the way of the Christ child to their threshold, and they place candles in their windows lest he miss his footing in the dark. In a small town near San Antonio, Texas, there is repeated each year, as it has been for close to a century, *"Los Pastores,"* the oldest folk play in Christendom. Many plantations throughout Texas put this play on with amateur casts, and it is seen every year at the San José Mission during Christmas week.

There is one typical California celebration of Christmastime, which is staged in a most spectacular location — the great Yosemite National Park. Here, where the echo of the great Yosemite waterfalls sounds in the ears, one of the great hotels of the park produces its dramatic spectacle. While dusk is falling over the tall trees of the park, bands of men dressed in white capped and cowled costumes to represent the ancient Druid hierarchy, gather from all directions, wending their way toward the celebration along different trails, plainly visible against the dark of the forest. They come singing carols, lighting their way with blazing torches. Chanting age-old melodies, they enter the great hall of the hotel, bearing with them an enormous yule log from the forest, twined with mistletoe. It is placed with ceremony in the great fireplace and lighted with a brand that has been treasured from the yule log of the previous year. The following night the remnants of the log, except for the brand saved for the coming year, are taken up the steep slopes and laid on a fire built at Glacier Point, high above the valley and the cascading waterfalls. Then, just as the last light fades from the western sky, the fire is pushed from the Point to become a flaming fireball that hisses and streaks down the mountainside to a ledge of rock hundreds of feet below. Thus at the edge of the Pacific ends the American Christmas Day, which had begun with Christmas Eve caroling to the chime of hand bells in the circling streets of Boston on the Atlantic seaboard, twenty-four hours before.

The holiday week is one of festivity that usually closes with New Year's parties and broken New Year's resolutions, but the great piece of medieval pageantry that is the Philadelphia Mummers' Parade rates a word for closing the week differently.

This spectacular affair is perhaps the oldest organized holiday celebration in our land, for its seeds were in the Viking festivals the Swedes introduced about 1650. Only the Pilgrims' annual Thanksgivings are older. The Swedish celebrations were noted for their unrestrained revelry. When the sober-minded Quakers came, they substituted something to take their place. This was a revival of the old English mummers' play with costumes and music and torchlights. Year after year, except in times of stress in the country, Philadelphia stages its annual pageantry. Even the Mardi gras — the Fat Tuesday celebrations — in New Orleans, do not outshine the opulence of the Philadelphia Mummers.

They represent clubs, many of them well into their second century of activity, whose members are from every trade and profession and every walk of life. The New Year's Mummer clubs spend all year preparing for the one day of their spectacular show. They are accompanied by string bands and are clad in fantastic costumes. Wearing gigantic headpieces, the "kings" of the so-called "dress" clubs walk up Philadelphia streets in proud array.

18. CHRISTMAS IN EUROPE

DRAWINGS BY DR. MIKLOS FOGHTUY

In many lands Christmas customs are interwoven with ancient folklore and legends that have been handed down from one generation to another. The Scandinavians have close ties with the Vikings, the Slavs dip deep into the rituals of the Greek Church; across the English Channel, the culture of the British Isles is grafted to the Druid faith. Christmas as we know it began when churches of Christ displaced the pagan gods, but we also intertwine some of the stories of the distant pagan past with the Christmas epics of the present. We have sorted out what we think are the most interesting customs that can easily be used for dramatization in Christmas pageants. Since Christmas in America is patterned after the Old English Christmas, we have described it in greater detail, so that it may be readily adapted to your Christmas festival or party for a large group.

In Spain, France, and Italy and neighboring countries, Christmas is set apart from other days of the year as one where the church services sound the keynote of the holiday. The holiday is what the word implies — holy day — the birthday of the Christ, the day of the Nativity. In each country, this day has its national characteristics, but fundamentally it is a day set aside for devotions and for mingling with the family.

Italy

In Italy, every house at Christmas time sets up the *preseptio,* the tiny version of the story of the Nativity. For weeks the markets display the miniature earthenware figures of the Holy Family, the Three Kings, the shepherds and their flocks, and all the

tiny angels with which to build the *presepito,* or manger, that means Christmas in Italian homes. Neighbors are with each other in making settings of the old, old story beautiful and true, some with a grotto where the Holy Family is grouped about the shining manger, with hills on which the shepherds watch their tiny sheep and across which the Three Kings may be seen riding from afar to bring their gifts of gold, frankincense, and myrrh to the Christ child.

The *ceppo* is an early Italian conception of a Christmas tree. It is a highly decorated structure with shelves that were filled with gifts and Nativity scenes. In some families there is a *ceppo* for every child.

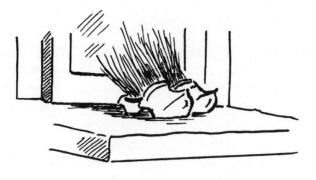

Spain

Across the blue Mediterranean, the same Latin customs have colored the celebrations of that land of festivals, Spain. No other country has so many "fiestas," as they are called, throughout the year. But the one at Christmas is the busiest and most elaborate. After attending church, the day is spent quietly at home. Later, all gather on the village square for merrymaking during the evening. It is customary to have an Urn of Fate, a large bowl in which all names are placed. From this they are drawn two at a time, and fate decides who shall be devoted friends for the year.

Then there is the ancient and probably pagan rite of "swinging the sun." Only the children perform it in these modern years. In Cadiz they still set up swings in the public squares, and the children vie to see which can go highest in the air to help old Sol begin his return journey northward.

The Twelfth-day is especially observed in Spanish lands, for it is the day that appeals to all with the love of the colorful and splendid in their natures. Traditionally, this is January 6, when the Magi, the Three Kings from the East, arrived to worship the Babe in the manger. The little children excitedly await the coming of Gaspar, Melchoir, and Balthasar, who travel up and down the land with gifts for good boys and girls. Before they go to sleep, the children stuff their shoes with straw and place them on balconies and in doorways, so the Kings' horses will have something to eat after their journey. In the morning, they are not surprised to find the straw gone and candy and gifts in the shoes instead.

125

In France, too, Christmas Day is a family affair with concentration on church attendance and worship. The celebrations begin the night before, on Christmas Eve. In every home the thrifty French mother brings out little figures and the miniature setting for the children to build a crèche — the French name for the Nativity scene, which we have adopted. Church bells peal out joyously at midnight, calling all to the celebration of the Christ Mass; the services are sure to be magnificent, with the splendid vestments shining in the glow of the altar candles. After mass, when everyone is back home, comes the *Réveillon*. To all French folk this means the most memorable meal of the year. The feast always includes *pâté de foie gras* and a special blood sausage, washed down with the local wine.

It is on Christmas Eve that French children set out their shoes before the fireplaces, expecting confidently that the good Père Noël, as they call the Christmas spirit, will fill them with nuts and sweets. In some of the provinces children wander through the village streets, singing old, old songs of the Noël and carrying a small crèche reverently at the head of the procession. They

stop at every door to give a holiday greeting, and hope for some *sous* as a reward.

Along the Riviera and the Côte D'Azur, especially in the older mountain towns, the old Nativity plays are presented before the altar each year. These have come down from medieval days, when this was the way the clergy told and retold the Christmas story.

It is New Year's Day that is set aside for general gift giving. The children try to rise early in the morning and surprise their parents with a hearty *"Bonne année,"* and from under a jacket or apron, produce little gifts they have made themselves.

Belgium

Saint Nicholas Day, December 6, is one of great happiness for the children in Belgium. They set up a tree and expect Saint Nicholas to fill it with gifts and good things to eat. He is depicted in a bishop's robes, wearing a miter and carrying a pas-toral staff. He is supposed to be riding a gray horse or white ass, so the children put out water, hay, carrots, and potatoes for it to eat. In the morning, the furniture is in general disorder, which shows that Saint Nicholas has been there, and in their shoes the children find sweetmeats and playthings if they have been good that year.

Switzerland

In Switzerland, Father Christmas is depicted as having a jovial red face and white beard, and he wears a long fur-trimmed robe. He marches through the villages with his wife Lucy. Lucy wears her hair in two long braids, and has a lace bodice and bright silk apron. She wears a round fur cap as she accompanies Father Christmas on his rounds; he distributes gifts to the boys, while she takes care of the girls.

In the French cantons of Switzerland, the Christ child, called the *Chriskindle,* makes the rounds of the village in a sleigh drawn by reindeer, carrying a load of candy and toys and Christmas cookies that are baked in fantastic shapes. The whole family goes to Midnight Mass at the church. Afterward, they go home to supper and tell anew the old wives' tales of Christmas miracles, when the dumb animals speak just at midnight; meanwhile the older folk peel onions gravely and throw the circles of peels to foretell the weather of the coming year. Singing carols, ringing cowbells, and yodeling their Noëls, the children of French Alpine villages go from door to door with their message of Noël, and their hands ready for the invariable housewives' gifts.

Christmas in Scandinavian Lands

Christmas celebrations in Scandinavian countries vary, but most of them reflect the original Viking strain.

Among the Danes, the greatest day of the yuletide festival is Christmas Eve. It begins early, on what is called "Little Christmas," December 23, and the gay celebrations last well into the New Year. On Little Christmas Day, the house is swept and garnished with holly and mistletoe, and all is finished by the time the church bells call people to worship. They have a midnight feast with roast goose, its apple and prune stuffing spilling out in rich gravy, red cabbage, white potatoes, followed by doughnuts

128

and cookies. Then comes that rich rice pudding called *"grot."* This is covered with sugar and sprinkled with cinnamon, and at the center is always a hole scooped out and filled with butter, the "eye" of the pudding. Just one almond is slipped into the pudding, and the lucky finder receives the almond gift, for which he must make a speech.

In Scandinavian countries no one is ever forgotten. Even the animals in the barns receive an extra ration, and a sheaf of wheat dipped in suet is hung in the crisp cold outside so that the birds, too, will have their Christmas. The sheaf is usual-ly mounted on a tall pole erected in the middle of the dooryard, and there is not a peasant in all Sweden who will sit down to dinner until he has first raised aloft a Christmas dinner for the birds that live in the snow.

In Denmark, church services are the or-der of the day during Christmas morning, and then homes, with windows shining and walls garlanded, are thrown wide open for guests that call during the twelve days of yuletide. On the table there is always food and drink for all comers, and let no one think to escape without partaking of the family hospitality. Something must be taken, be shared, if it be but a crumb or a sip, for the guest who goes away without breaking his host's bread takes away the house-hold "yule" — their luck for the coming year.

It is at Christmas time that the "little people" visit all the Scandinavian countries. They are tiny gnomelike figures whose images appear in decorations as symbols of the holiday season. They are always found in family groups, with grandparents, parents, and wee babies, who come to stay among humanity at the yuletide. It is said that they make their permanent quarters in barns, on farms, and in villages, and one sometimes hears them creeping over floors of attics or up and down stairs. It is considered lucky to have such a family come to stay, and every household so honored remembers their little guests on Christmas Eve. They always provide them with their Christmas dinner, and every family carries a great bowl steaming with hot milk out to the barn or up to the attic and leaves it for the fairy guests. No one ever sees them drink it, but the children always find it has been licked clean during the night.

On Christmas Eve, the church bells ring, the shops close, and, they say, Christmas peace descends on every home. There are the long smörgasbord tables prepared with dozens of appetizers and in the kitchen a kettle simmers with the traditional *molje*. This is the rich pot liquor in which all the Christmas meats have been cooked. Each member of the family begins the celebrations by dipping into it bits of Norwegian flat bread and wishing everyone a "Merry Christmas" as he eats it. The housewives also prepare their Christmas cod, called "lutefish" — a clear, trembling jelly-like dish served with white butter sauce and whole white potatoes.

The Swedish folk begin their festivities early on December 13, which is called Saint Lucia's Day. This is the day that starts when a young daughter of the house, who has been chosen for the role, slips out of bed before the household wakes and garbs herself in the traditional costume of the Lucia Bride. It is a soft, long white robe, belted with the silver belt of family brides. On her head, she places the crown of shining lingonberry leaves, and twelve small upright candles. She wakes her smaller brothers and goes to the kitchen to prepare the morning coffee. The boys put on traditional baker's caps, light the candles, and help fill breadbaskets with sweet rolls and cakes. The twelve candles signify each day of the Christmas season, which begins on Christmas Eve.

Everyone must arise early to attend Christmas Mass and all along the way lighted candles in farmhouse windows brighten the path. On all the heights of Norway and Sweden, great bonfires burn to honor the birth of the Christ child, and they show bright and clear during the long winter nights.

In Sweden, *Jule-nisen* brings gifts to the boys and girls. He is a red-clad figure with a pointed cap and long white beard, who lives in a stable during the year. At midnight there is a commotion outside the door, and into the room he comes astride a goat, bringing gifts for everyone.

The staunchly independent people of Finland have some special customs all their own, and one of these is the steam bath that tradition rules everyone must take on Christmas Eve. Christmas morning begins with church services, and then the merrymaking and feasting start; they last until after the New Year. On that day calls are paid to old and new friends; January 6 is celebrated as the end of yuletide, when the tree is dismantled and the holiday terminates in a mad rush of singing and dancing.

CHRISTMAS AMONG THE SLAVIC PEOPLE

Although Christmas is frowned upon in Communist-controlled countries, most of the customs are still kept in the homes, particularly in rural areas where older generations remember the past. In some regions the peasants go about the countryside masked as the animals — cows, pigs, sheep, etc. — in the story of the manger. They sing the story of the miraculous birth at Bethlehem, and in return are rewarded with gifts.

Usually the priest makes his round of the parish and blesses the Christmas candles for the home. Everyone watches the sky eagerly to see the first star, and then gather together inside their homes to eat a Christmas supper. Holiday wishes are exchanged and hay decorates the table to remind all of the humble birth of the Child.

133

In Poland each child writes a letter telling what he wants for Christmas. The letter is placed on the window sill where the Wise Men can get at it easily. On the evening of December 24, when the first star appears in the eastern skies, the family gathers for the *Wilia supper*. Straw is scattered under the tablecloth, and one chair is left vacant for the Holy Child. Before sitting down to the table, all members of the household break the traditional *oplatek* — a thin unleavened wafer — and exchange good wishes. The *oplatek* is known as the "bread of love." The wafers are sent by mail to the absent members of the family. Because Christmas Eve is a fast day in Poland, the *Wilia* supper consists of elaborate fish and vegetable dishes, served in seven, nine, or eleven courses. After the meal, the family gathers about the Christmas tree and the traditional carols (*koledy*) are sung. Gifts are not exchanged because Polish children receive their presents on the Feast of St. Nicholas (December 6). Around midnight the family leaves the home to attend the *Pasterka* (shepherd's mass) in churches throughout Poland. All along the highways, Nativity scenes are set in the snow to remind the traveler that Christ was born in Bethlehem.

December 31 is St. Sylvester's Eve, and on this night one does anything one wishes between twelve and one. No law obtains, so everyone is his own master.

Bulgarians and Romanians begin their festivities with the first star on Christmas Eve. The parish priests have toured the districts and blessed the homes and animals for the coming year. The people have been observing two weeks of fasting, but when the star appears, candles are lighted on a table laden with festive foods. They burn a cube of incense and then the head of the household holds a loaf of bread high over his head and prays that his wheat will grow as tall as the height of that loaf. Each guest at the table breaks a piece from the loaf; it is said that luck will go with the person who pulls the biggest piece.

In Romania, starting on Christmas night, boys go from house to house, singing carols, reciting poetry, and repeating the Christmas story. The leader of the group carries a large star, called *steana,* made of wood and mounted on a long pole. It is covered with gilt paper and colored streamers on which are fastened small bells that hang down or float in the wind. A picture of the Holy Family is painted or pasted in the center, and to make it glow, a small candle is placed inside.

SAINT NICHOLAS COUNTRIES

The Christmas spirit of the Teutonic lands goes by the name of Good Saint Nicholas, the story of whom is found elsewhere in this book (*see* pages 159-162). All these countries begin this season of good cheer on December 6, which is known as St. Nicholas Day. In all these places he is represented as a tall, venerable, kind-faced man with a beard, wearing the cape of the bishop and the miter headdress. With him one finds the young dark-skinned partner known as Black Peter, who always carries a bunch of switches. Of course, Saint Nicholas rewards the good children by giving them gifts from the bag he carries, while Black Peter distributes switches to the parents of bad boys and girls.

In Germany, Saint Nicholas is an advanced messenger of Christmas, and the actual gifts are not delivered until Christmas Eve. Sometimes these gifts come from the hands of the Christmas Man, and in other sections, it is *Christ Kindle,* the Christ child himself, who gives them. He is said to wander through the snows of Christmas Eve with presents for old and young.

The weeks between St. Nicholas Day and Christmas are the times for the great fairs in Germany and are often called *doms* from the fact that they were held in the squares before the cathedrals. There, booths are filled with tempting toys, with cookies and gingerbread men in all shapes and colors, and the festivities last into the Christmas week. The Christmas tree is undoubtedly the German contribution of this decorative feature to many lands. It was not a part of the English yuletide until Queen Victoria's prince consort, a German, sought to bring it from his homeland to their children.

There are some interesting sidelights in the celebrations that mark the Christmas season in Hungary, the land of the Magyars, with their mirth and melody, their picturesque costumes and fascinating folk tales and dances. Here, as in other middle European lands, the season opens with Saint Nicholas and his day, on December 6. The actual Christmas festivities, however, begin at school on Christmas Eve. There, before the classes are dismissed, the children gather in a circle and each recites a verse of the Bible story of the Nativity. They sing carols and each child is presented with a bag of sweets, all prepared by a group of parents so that everyone receives the same. When they reach home they find the door to the best room or parlor is closed and they must wait until a bell is rung and the door thrown open to reveal the lighted Christmas tree, real candles burning brightly amid its dark-green boughs. Underneath the tree are the fascinating gifts, all unwrapped so that the children see at once if Saint Nicholas has fulfilled his promise to bring the sled or the skis or the skates or doll. Before they touch the gifts, the children embrace their parents, then join in a ring around the tree and sing Christmas carols, and voicing their thanks to the Christ child who brings the gifts to Hungarian homes.

After the gifts have been enjoyed, supper is announced. The favorite Hungarian Christmas dessert is a special pastry, made of a rich piecrust rolled very thin and covered with a paste that is a mixture of finely chopped walnuts blended with sugar and just enough milk so that it spreads. This is rolled up and baked. For

138

breakfast Christmas morning there is always the special treat of a bread called milk bread, traditionally eaten at that meal.

Church services follow on Christmas Day, with all the family attending. On the way home, they stop at friends to offer the greetings of the season, but December 25 is a real home day, and just the family gathers round to enjoy the Christmas dinner. The following day, however, is called the second Christmas, and then the merrymaking begins with parties and festivities among the circle of family friends.

Throughout Hungary, in the villages and rural areas, the actual merrymaking begins a week before Christmas Eve. Children dressed as kings and shepherds, and carefully bearing a small Nativity scene, wander through the countryside and from door to door in the villages. They sing and tell the Christmas story, and are rewarded by householders wherever they stop. After church services on Christmas Eve in the towns and villages, the shepherds come down from the hills, and standing in the central squares, they crack their long whips and blow on the great long calling horns that they use to summon their flocks.

There is a special candy that the Hungarians make at Christmas time from a fondant base which they cut in pieces and roll in bright-colored papers. They twist the ends and fringe the paper, then hang the candies as baubles on the Christmas tree.

SANTAS IN EUROPE

19. SAVE YOUR CHRISTMAS CARDS

Every year many people ask themselves, "What can I do with my Christmas cards? There are so many beautiful ones. I can't bear to throw them away."

Here is a suggestion that may appeal to you, particularly if you expect to give drama productions or assist arts and crafts groups throughout the year.

Why not mount your Christmas cards in a large scrapbook, to be used as source material for activity clubs? Once you have such a book, you will be amazed to find how often it is used by different groups. The cards will provide ideas for costumes, stage sets, arts and crafts designs, and numerous other needs that arise in a community center. Such a book requires a careful selection of subject material from hundreds of cards. So ask your friends to save their cards for you and others who are interested in the community program.

First, you will need a strong cover for your book (you must decide the size). Three-ply fir wood is perhaps the most satisfactory; it is inexpensive and will not warp as readily as plain wood. You might stain it with oil, then give it several coats of shellac, smoothing it each time with steel wool. When it is completely dry, polish it by applying floor wax and rubbing with a soft rag.

Cut a strip about two inches wide from the left side of the top cover, about a half-inch from the edge, and hinge it with metal hinges to the left side of the cover so that it may be raised. If you wish, you may use scrap leather. Bore several holes in the two-inch strip with matching holes in the left side of the back cover so they may be laced together with a leather thong or heavy cord.

Ordinary brown wrapping paper makes an excellent filler for a scrapbook. It is thin, yet tough enough to be handled, and it provides a neutral-colored background for the cards. Cut the pages about a half-inch smaller than the cover. Punch holes corresponding with those in the binding and reinforce them with gummed circles sold at the ten-cent stores. Paper cement is most satisfactory for mounting the cards, as they can be removed easily when you wish to replace some of them with better subjects. Label the different sections of your book according to the subjects you wish to use. Here are a few suggestions:

COSTUMES

You will find many folk costumes on foreign cards, particularly from Sweden, Switzerland, Poland, Holland, and Mexico. The Swedish cards show the native dress of the different provinces and also many of their Christmas customs.

Period Costumes. Many cards depict scenes of old Christmas customs such as bringing in the yule log, serving the boar's head, or drinking wassail, and the people are usually dressed in the traditional costumes. You may also find costume suggestions for minstrels or carol singers. They may not always be authentic, but they are interesting and effective.

Costumes for Tableaux

Many of the religious scenes such as the Nativity or the coming of the Wise Men make excellent source material for tableaux. Construct a large frame and pose characters as they are shown in the picture while someone tells the story of the scene. This is a suggestion for Sunday evening programs throughout the year.

Fancy Costumes for parties, masquerades, and plays may also be found. Save any cards that have a character dressed in an unusual costume. You may find a need for it before the year is over.

Poster Suggestions. You will undoubtedly find a number of cards that suggest ideas for posters. Even though you do not use the actual subjects shown on the cards, they suggest layouts, color schemes, lettering, and characters for novel posters. Many lend themselves to a three-dimensional design for large posters to be hung in hallways or big rooms.

Design for Metalwork. The novel candlesticks, metal bowls, lamp bases, and lanterns should be a stimulus for new designs in the metal shop. There are many suggested designs, too, for wrought-iron work such as candleholders, hinges for doorways, and irons for fireplaces. If you have a metal shop, all such cards deserve a space in your book.

Other Uses — Animals. Sometime during the year you are going to want an animal picture, and it is often surprising how hard it is to find a picture of a particular animal on the spur of the moment. Among the animals most commonly found on Christmas cards are dogs of all kinds, horses, reindeer, polar bears, lambs, cats, and many other pets that are often photographed by their owners.

143

During the past few years there has been a tendency to show pictures of stuffed animals on "comic" Christmas cards. You might find pictures of elephants, pandas, bears, dogs, and many you cannot name. All these become suggestions for puppet characters, bazaars, toys, or dolls.

Craft Designs. Any card showing an unusual design should be placed in a section set aside for the arts and crafts classes. Many of the cards now have colorful peasant designs for borders or as a part of the decoration. Indian designs are also used, particularly in the West and Southwest. There are always a number of pictures that suggest cut paper designs or houses and furniture that may be made from paper for the activity program.

There are usually some cards made by craftsmen. These sometimes suggest new methods of using such techniques as finger painting, etching, silk screens, or spatter printing. Many of the suggestions may be adopted to party invitations, greeting cards for various seasons, party favors, dance programs, and similar uses.

Nature Designs. It is hard to find in a limited nature library pictures of many of the greens shown on Christmas cards — holly, mistletoe, poinsettias, and the different evergreens. There are occasional suggestions for flower arrangements and numerous ideas for decorating doorways, windows, or mantels that might be adapted to the different seasons.

As you look over your cards and divide them according to subjects, you will think of other uses. There will be many duplicate cards and others that you will not want to use, so why not recondition them and make them into scrapbooks for hospitals? Remove the soiled spots with an artgum eraser, and eliminate writing with ink eradicator.

Card Transformations

This makes an excellent party game for anyone, be they young or old. Try to fit small bodies onto large heads, or vice versa — or you may suggest placing a large figure in a miniature setting or making a dwarf by selecting houses and trees that are too large. Provide guests with scissors and paste and offer prizes.

Christmas Tags and Seals

Before throwing away your Christmas cards, look at them carefully and see if a portion of the design would be suitable for making a Christmas tag or seal. For a tag, the cutout should be rectangular or square — such as is usually found on Christmas packages. Punch a small hole at one end, thread through a double loop of thin red string, and you will be ready to label your gifts the following year. Likewise, cut out small motifs and store them in small envelopes.

Fun with Christmas Cards

Children can play with Christmas cards by cutting out various parts and arranging them into story-telling sets, peep shows, etc. Turn a cardboard box upside down and punch holes or cut a slit wherever a cutout is to be placed, as shown in the illustration. If the characters are large enough, paste them to a heavy strip of cardboard or a match in order to make them stand up straight. The children will enjoy inventing stories of their own, and since Christmas cards have all sorts of characters, trees, houses, animals, etc., they will not be lacking in subject matter.

To impart seeming life to little figures painted on Christmas cards is a performance little children will enjoy. Cut a hole large enough for the forefinger to protrude and paint a face either on the tip or a finger from a glove. Floral cards can have nodding fairies peering out from among the petals, or if you have a picture of a house, it will be amusing to thrust a little head, wearing a nightcap, looking for Santa Claus.

Angels We Have Heard

Angels we have heard on high,
Sweetly singing o'er our plains,
And the mountains in reply
Echoing their joyous strains.
Gloria in excelsis Deo, Gloria in excelsis Deo.

In the fields, beside their sheep,
Shepherds watching thro' the night,
Hear, amid the silence deep,
Those sweet voices, clear and bright.
Gloria in excelsis Deo, Gloria in excelsis Deo.

Joyful hearts with one accord,
Spread the tidings far and wide:
Born to us is Christ the Lord,
At this happy Christmas tide.
Gloria in excelsis Deo, Gloria in excelsis Deo.

ANONYMOUS

20. CHRISTMAS CLASSICS

A beautiful family custom is that of having some of the immortal Christmas stories read aloud in the family circle on Christmas Eve. Some families keep the Christmas classics in a box or a special bookcase.

Mary Gould Davis, for years in charge of storytelling at the New York Public Library, suggests the following tales for a family Christmas list. She has found that children like to have these stories read and told to them over and over.

The Christ Child, as told by St. Matthew and St. Luke, illustrated by Maud and Miska Petersham (New York: Doubleday & Co.).

The Christmas Carol, by Charles Dickens. (Published in several editions.)

Christmas Carols, illustrated and put into simple music by Grace Castagnetta and Hendrik Willem Van Loon (New York: Simon & Schuster).

Come Christmas, by Eleanor Farjeon, decorated by Rachel Field (Philadelphia: Frederick A. Stokes).

"The Elves and the Shoemaker," in *Household Stories of the Brothers Grimm* (New York: The Macmillan Co.).

"The Fir Tree," in Hans Christian Andersen, *Fairy Tales and Legends*, ed. by Rex Whistler (New York: The Macmillan Co.).

"The Good Night," in Ruth Sawyer, *The Long Christmas* (New York: The Viking Press).

"*Now the Good Gifts Were Used by Two*," in Howard Pyle, *The Wonder Clock* (New York: Harper & Brothers).

The Velveteen Rabbit, by Margery Bianco (New York: Doubleday & Co.).

The Well of the Star, by Elizabeth Goudge (New York: Coward-McCann).

Saint Nicholas, in Eleanor Farjeon, *The Saints* (New York: Oxford University Press).

If you want a full book of Christmas classics, we recommend *The Home Book of Christmas,* edited by May Lamberton Becker (New York: Dodd, Mead & Co.). The order of contents follows the great events of the holiday festival — The Shepherds, The Magi, The Preparations, The Waits, The Gifts, Santa Claus, The Tree, and many of the old carols.

Here are a few of our favorite classics we think are suitable for reading aloud either at a public gathering or in the family circle. We are sorry not to include others equally beautiful, but our space is limited.

Ye Great Astonishment

Whosoever on ye nighte of ye nativity of ye young Lord Jesus, in ye great snows, shall fare forth bearing a succulent bone for ye loste and lamenting hounde, a whisp of hay for ye shivering horse, a cloak of warm rainment for ye stranded wayfarer, a bundle of fagots for ye twittering crone, a flagon of red wine for him whose marrow withers, a garland of bright berries for one who has worn chains, gay arias of lute and harp for all huddled birds who thought that song was dead, and divers lush sweetmeats for such babes' faces as peer from lonely windows —

To him shall be proffered and returned gifts of such an astonishment as will rival the hues of the peacock and the harmonies of heavens so that though he live to ye greate age when man goes stooping and querulous because of the nothing that is left in him, yet shall he walk upright and remembering, as one whose heart shines like a great star in his breasts.

SOURCE UNKNOWN

The Storke

A Christmas Ballad
(From the flyleaf of an Edward VI prayer book — 1549)

The Storke she rose on Christmas Eve
    And sayed unto her broode,
I now must fare to Bethlehem
    To viewe the Sonne of God.

She gave to eche his dole of mete,
    She stowed them fayrlie in,
And faire she flew and faste she flew,
    And came to Bethlehem.

Now where is He of David's line?
    She asked at House and Halle,
He is not here, they spake hardlye,
    But in the maungier stalle.

She found Hym in the maungier stalle
    With that most Hoyle Mayde;
The gentyle Storke shee wept to see
    The Lord so rudelye layde.

Then from her panntynge brest she plucked
    The fethers whyte and warm;
She strawed them in the maungier bed
    To keep the Lord from harm.

Now blessed bee the gentyle Storke
    Forever more quothe hee,
For that she saw My sadde estate,
    And showed Pytye.

Full welcom shall shee ever bee
    In hamlet and in halle,
And hight [called] henceforth the Blessed Byrd
    And friend of babyes all.

A Christmas Prayer

By Henry St. George Tucker, D.D.

In this hour of storm and danger we remember with true penitence, O God, the manifold sins which have drawn us apart from Thee and which have added to the pain of our fellow men.

For contentment with prosperity and for the love of comfort which dreads the cost of serving Thee;

For unbrotherly neglect of our neighbor's needs in forgetfulness that we are members one of another;

For letting class divisions mar the unity of our people;

For race prejudice;

For the self-centered blindness which ignores the claims of world fellowship;

For being proud of ourselves and forgetful of Thee;

O Lord, forgive us.

In spite of the sins for which we repent, O God, Thy gifts to us are many and great. In the midst of uncertainty and peril we have good cause for gratitude to Thee.

For our inheritance of freedom, never more precious than today;

For all that is sound and true in the life of our country — for whatever in our homes, our communities, our industries and our government bears Thy mark and is in accordance with Thy will;

For the opportunity that still is ours to bear a brave part in sharing the world's burdens; We thank Thee, O Lord.

Thou has taught us, O Lord, that except Thou dost keep the city, the watchman waketh but in vain. Knowing that Thou art the strength of all those who put their trust in Thee, we offer these our petitions:

That whatever is weak and self-indulgent and self-satisfied may be purged from our lives;

That we may count the liberty bequeathed by our forefathers as a heritage to be fearlessly maintained;

That the kingdoms of this world may become Thy Kingdom, where Christ shall reign forever and ever;

We beseech Thee, O Lord.

A Prayer of Saint Francis of Assisi

Lord, make me a channel of Thy peace —
That where there is hatred — I may bring love —
That where there is wrong, I may bring the spirit
                            of forgiveness —
That where there is discord, I may bring harmony —
That where there is error — I may bring truth —
That where there is doubt, I may bring faith —
That where there is despair, I may bring hope —
That where there are shadows, I may bring Thy light —
That where there is sadness — I may bring joy —
Lord, grant that I may seek rather to comfort
                     than to be comforted —
To understand — than to be understood,
To love — than to be loved:
For — it is by giving — that one receives —
It is by self-forgetting, that one finds;
It is by forgiving — that one is forgiven:
It is by dying — that one awakens to eternal life.

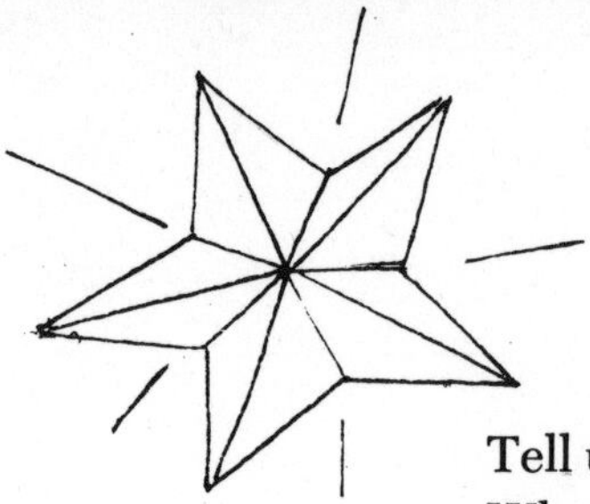

The Star Song

Tell us, thou clear and heavenly tongue,
Where is the Babe that lately sprung?
Lies He the lily-beds among?

Or say, if this new birth of ours
Sleeps, laid within some ark of flowers,
Spangles with dew-light? thou canst clear
All doubts, and manifest the where.

Declare to us, bright star, if we shall seek
Him in the morning's blushing cheek,
Or search the beds of spices through,
To find Him out?

Star

No, this ye need not do;
But only come and see him rest,
A Princely Babe, in's mother's breast.

Chorus

He's seen! He's seen! why then around,
Let's kiss the sweet and holy ground;
And all rejoice that we have found
A King, before conception, crowned.

Come then, come then, and let us bring
Unto our pretty twelfth-tide King,
Each one his several offering.

Chorus

And when night comes we'll give Him wassailing;
And that His treble honors may be seen,
We'll choose Him King, and make His mother queen.

ROBERT HERRICK

156

Bells

I heard the bells on Christmas day,
Their old familiar carols play,
And wild and sweet the words repeat
Of "Peace on earth, good will to men!"

And thought how, as the day had come,
The belfries of all Christendom
Had rolled along th' unbroken song,
Of "Peace on earth, good will to men!"

And in despair I bowed my head;
"There is no peace on earth," I said,
"For hate is strong and mocks the song
Of peace on earth, good will to men!"

Then pealed the bells more loud and deep;
"God is not dead; nor doth He sleep!
The wrong shall fail, the right prevail,
With peace on earth, good will to men!"

HENRY WADSWORTH LONGFELLOW

Bells

What a world of merriment their melody foretells!
  How they tinkle, tinkle, tinkle, in the icy air of night!
While the stars that over sparkle
All the heavens seem to twinkle
  With a crystalline delight;
  Keeping time, time, time,
  In a sort of Runic rhyme,
To the tintinnabulation that so musically wells
From the bells, bells, bells, bells, bells, bells, bells —
From the jingling and the tinkling of the bells.
From poem by EDGAR ALLEN POE

Christmas Song

Why do bells for Christmas ring?
Why do little children sing?

Once a lovely shining star,
Seen by shepherds from afar,
Gently moved until its light
Made a manger-cradle bright.

There a darling Baby lay
Pillowed soft upon the hay.
And his mother sang and smiled,
This is Christ, the Holy Child.

So the bells for Christmas ring,
So the little children sing.
LYDIA A. C. WARD

Saint Nicholas — The Christmas Saint

Saint Nicholas, a man of rare modesty, was born in the latter part of the third century. His birthplace was Patara, a town in the province of Lycia in Asia Minor. Unlike most of the saints, his birth was far from humble. His parents were rich, and one of his uncles was an archbishop. He came in answer to the prayers of his mother and father, and it is said that when the nurse was about to give him his first bath, the infant stood on his feet in his tub and, with his hands joined in prayer and his eyes raised to heaven, was entranced for the space of two hours.

His first miracle was one of kindness. When he was going to school, he met a crippled woman in the street and looked on her with such love and tenderness that immediately she became well and strong and walked free.

159

His uncle saw that he was destined for a life of sanctity and good works, so he sent him to a monastery, where he became a priest. Nicholas never sought honors, but his wisdom and virtue were so great that he could not avoid them. He became superior of the monastery at an early age, and in a few years he was made an archbishop.

An epidemic carried away his father and mother when he was only twenty, and he inherited all their great wealth. But fortune had no appeal for him, and he gave it away as fast as he could. You will notice that he is always pictured holding three purses of gold. That is to remind us of one of his many kindly deeds. A poor man had three daughters whom he was about to sell in the slave market, for he found it impossible to get together the dowries without which they could not marry, and he could no longer provide for them. Many a saint would have overlooked a circumstance like this, but not Saint Nicholas. When he learned the pitiful story, he went by night and tossed three purses of gold through the poor father's window, and the girls were thus saved from slavery. The grateful man did not rest until he had found the benefactor, who begged him not to tell, but fortunately there are many people who like to tell about good deeds, and so the story has come down to us.

The thoughts of Archbishop Nicholas were so pure and unselfish that he often knew when people needed aid without being told. Once three little boys who had strayed some distance from their homes fell into the hands of a wicked butcher who slew them and put their bodies into a tub of brine. Nicholas was led to pass that way, and knowing within himself that a crime had been committed, he went inside and terrified the wicked butcher by restoring the children to life before his very eyes.

Another time three rich students were killed by an innkeeper who wanted their money, and Saint Nicholas brought them back to life. It is small wonder that he is the patron of children and students.

160

He stilled a storm at sea one night when it threatened to over-whelm a ship, and the sailors could never be certain whether he was on the ship in person or not; they saw him, to be sure, but when they put into the port of Myra to go to church and thank God for delivering them, there was Archbishop Nicholas at the altar. He would take no credit to himself, but seafaring men ever since have invoked Nicholas as their patron in time of danger. One of the very first Dutch ships to enter what is now New York harbor carried a figure of Saint Nicholas at her masthead.

On several occasions Nicholas jeopardized his own life by be-friending men who had been wrongly accused, and there are folks who say it is well to remember this saint if one is under false condemnation, for they feel that he surely remembers in heaven those whose troubles touched his heart when he was on earth.

In his crowded lifetime he had, in fact, time for everyone and everything that needed to be done, but not for himself. He even attended the Council of Nicaea in 325 A.D., when the Nicene Creed was composed to attest faith in the deity of Christ.

When he had grown very old and tired, he was told in a vision that he was to be allowed to rest from his labors in behalf of mankind. He said farewell to his people and retired to the mon-astery where he had begun his ecclesiastical life. He received the Sacraments of his church and waited with joy to leave this world. It was on December 6 that he departed, and the monks who were assembled around him all declared that they saw with their own eyes a throng of patriarchs, saints, angels, and archangels who came to carry him to his home in heaven.

He is buried in the town of Bari, in southern Italy, and there they remember him on May 7, because it was on that day that his remains were brought to Bari from Asia Minor. Why, it is hard to say, for he belongs particularly to the eastern church. Everywhere else he is specially remembered in the church services on De-cember 6.

When the Dutch came to America, they brought with them

161

their love and recollection of Saint Nicholas, and at Christmas time the early Knickerbockers would put flowers before a figure of a gentle old man in bishop's robes and miter. Gradually, however, no one knows just how or when, his benevolence and his love of children were given prominence and his miracles faded from general memory; in place of the archbishop there emerged the jolly character we know and love as Santa Claus (San Nicholaus). But we must not forget that his descriptive title is *thaumaturgus,* which means the "wonder worker," for that he was in all truth.

(Children could make a good Christmas play from this story.)

Hand-dipped Christmas Candles

As a prelude to an old-fashioned Christmas, many families enjoy making their own Christmas candles. All who share in the activity will learn to revere our ancestors, who accomplished so much by candlelight, and made all the candles themselves.

Paraffin, tallow, and candle wicking will be needed, and some tall containers (olive bottles and tall cookie tins) to hold the molten wax, and a container for hot water to keep wax melted while working. Perhaps someone you know has a candle mold, which lessens the work considerably. Star cookie molds can be used effectively.

If tallow is used, it must be "tried out" or melted, and if it contains any foreign matter, it should be strained through cheesecloth. Use an old tin can, bent to make a snout, from which to pour, for tallow is hard to remove from a vessel. Use the same can for heating and pouring the wax.

To dip candles:—

Get your wicks ready first. Seven-ply candle wicking, which can be purchased at hardware or ten-cent stores, is a good size. For a wick which will stand upright and burn slowly, braid the candle wicking, since it is hard to twist tight enough by hand. Melt the tallow and pour it into the tall jars or cans. Dip the braided wicks into the molten tallow, holding them until the wax is set so that it will not run or flatten when laid down. After the first dipping has set, dip again; keep on coating the wicks until the candles are the thickness you want. Getting a candle an inch in diameter takes about twenty-five dips — so one determined folk-crafter learned.

A mold simplifies everything. There is a hole at the bottom of each section for the wick. Use fine spool wire, (about five inches looped over) for pulling the wicking through the fine holes, and knot it underneath the molds so that it will stay in place. Use hairpins or the same spool wire for holding the wicks straight at the top while pouring. Melt the tallow and pour a little in; when it begins to set, fill the mold. This prevents the tallow from oozing out of the bottom. Hang the candles up to cool, and cool them slowly and thoroughly so that they won't crack. To remove candles from mold, first heat the sides of the mold slightly by dipping it in hot water or wrapping around it a hot damp cloth so that the candles are not marred. As we said in the beginning, making "tallow dips" and "hand-dipped" candles is no small matter. But it is fun, especially when getting ready for Christmas.

If any of the family become proficient, they might essay a very large decorated candle. This is an enterprise calling for artistry and patience, but the results can be wonderful.

Melt some paraffin into which several crayons have been added for color, and while still warm, beat with a dower egg beater. Pour the foamy substance over the hardened candle, allowing it to drip over the sides. The designs can also be carved on a large candle by using carving tools.

Santa's Reindeer

The moon, on the breast of the new-fallen snow,
Gave the lustre of midday to objects below;
When, what to my wondering eyes should appear,
But a miniature sleigh, and eight tiny reindeer,
With a little old driver, so lively and quick,
I knew in a moment it must be St. Nick.
More rapid than eagles his coursers they came,
And he whistled, and shouted, and called them by name:
"Now, Dasher! now, Dancer! now, Prancer and Vixen!
On, Comet! on, Cupid! on, Donder and Blitzen!
To the top of the porch! to the top of the wall!
Now dash away! dash away! dash away all!"

From *A Visit from St. Nicholas,* by CLEMENT C. MOORE

21. CHRISTMAS CAROLS

"God rest you merry, gentlemen," comes floating clear through frosty air on Christmas Eve, along hawthorne-bordered hedges, through narrow winding streets of English countryside and town. Each year, even in this mid-twentieth-century, an age-old custom is repeated anew as the lilting melody of yesteryear pours from the throats of English folk of all ages. The English Christmas waits are following tradition. They greet Christmas with joyous song — "Let nothing you dismay!" fades over the hills where yuletide seems most at home.

Across the stormy Channel, little French boys and girls wander through the streets of French villages and towns all the way from the stern coast of Brittany to the mimosa-laden air of the Côte d'Azur, and they, too, are singing on Christmas Eve. "Noël, Noël," comes in childish trebles as they go from house to house, echoing that first carol of two thousand years ago. Far to the north, in Scandinavian lands, bands of young lads move about the mountainsides, their way lit in the eerie darkness of the Arctic night by torches that they hold blazing aloft as they follow their leader, the star bearer. Singing, as they go, the tale of the Christ child born in Bethlehem, echoing from crag and mountain fiords. High above on the same rocky peaks blaze bonfires like those lit by the Vikings of old, their forefathers, in their pagan defiance of the demons of the dark winter that had devoured their sun. Over the scene the streaks of eerie northern lights flash vividly in rainbow-hued splendor.

South and east, music resounds on Christmas Eve. It is heard in Italy, in Spain, across the Alps in Switzerland, Germany, and Austria. All over western Europe sonorous melody rings out in the still night. In this joyous caroling listeners remember that first Christ Mass sung by the heavenly host to the music of the spheres when the Christ child was born.

This music of rejoicing goes back further than the two thousand years since the birth of Christ. Some of the qualities of Greece in her glory and of Rome before her greatness declined and much of the deep-toned chanting of the old Hebrew music form part of the tradition of the carols. With the coming of the Christian era, all this musical art of the past was blended into the carols. Ancient traditions gave birth to and nurtured carol singing, for the early Christians had no other musical form. Song and dance had been the age-old accompaniments of ancient religious ceremonies. Through them, gratitude to the gods was expressed and prayers for favor and protection were offered. But the ancient oracles had lost the authority of their voice. Glowing anew on the ashes of the dead pagan fires were the sparks of a new world faith, kindled by the warmth of this new and personal devotion. The carols are old yet ever new.

Across the wide Atlantic spread the traditions of carol singing. Radio and television spur on the renewals year by year. The tolling of Big Ben in London, ushering in Christmas Day there, is echoed a few hours later by Trinity Church in New York, and then, hour by hour, the sound moves with the growing day across the mountains, the deep valleys, and the rolling prairies. And as it does, our land resounds with the old familiar carols.

Now 'tis Christmas Time

Traditional
Västergötland, Sweden

Nu är det Jul - i - gen, Nu är det Jul - i - gen, Och

ef - ter Jul så kom-mer Pås - ka.   O   det var in - te sant, O

det var in - te sant, För   ef - ter Jul så kom-mer Fas - ta!

Words:

1. Now 'tis Christmas time, now 'tis Christmas time,
   And Christmas time will last till Easter;
2. Now 'tis Easter time, now 'tis Easter time,
   And Easter time will last till Christmas.

Formation:

Couples in sets of four abreast facing other fours at about ten feet. Sets are numbered one or two.

Step:

A light running step.

Action:

1. Set Number One, run forward 6 steps and back 5 steps, during the words "Now 'tis Christmas time, now 'tis Christmas time, and Christmas time will last till Easter."
2. Same is repeated by set Number Two.
1. Each set of four does a circle to the left (12 counts — turn on word "Easter").
2. Each set of four, circle to right.
1. Each set of eight (one set Number One and opposite set Number Two) circle left as above.
2. The circle is repeated to right.

167

1. Each set of four forms a pinwheel with right hands joined, move clockwise, 12 steps.
2. Each set of four repeats the pinwheel with left hands joined, move counterclockwise 12 steps.
1. Repeat with pinwheel of eight, ladies form pinwheel, men walk beside partners, arms linked.
2. All face about, repeat with ladies' left hands joined.
1. and (2) repeated indefinitely.

Weaving. First player of each top set now leads his set with hands joined around behind the second set, in front of the third, and so on, making a loop at the end of the line, and coming to rest at end of line, in the same order as at the start. This leaves a new top set.

Repeat from very beginning until all sets have been at top.

(Reprinted from *Musical Mixers and Simple Square Dances* by courtesy of the National Recreation Association, 315 Fourth Avenue, N. Y.)

A Christmas Carol

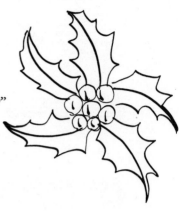

"What means this glory round our feet,"
   The Magi mused, "more bright than morn?"
And voices chanted clear and sweet,
   "Today the Prince of Peace is born!"

"What means that star," the Shepherds said,
   "That brightens through the rocky glen?"
And angels, answering overhead,
   Sang, "Peace on earth, good-will to men!"

"Tis eighteen hundred years and more
   Since those sweet oracles were dumb;
We wait for Him, like them of yore;
   Alas, He seems so slow to come!

But it was said in words of gold,
   No time or sorrow e'er shall dim,
That little children might be bold
   In perfect trust to come to Him.

All round about our feet shall shine
   A light like that the wise men saw,
If we our loving wills incline
   To that sweet Life which is the Law.

So shall we learn to understand
   The simple faith of shepherds then,
And, clasping kindly hand in hand,
   Sing, "Peace on earth, good-will to men!"

But they who do their souls no wrong,
   But keep at eve the faith of morn,
Shall daily hear the angel-song
   "Today the Prince of Peace is born!"

JAMES RUSSELL LOWELL

WHAT SHINES ON THE MOUNTAIN

Ancient Jugoslav

1. What shines on the— moun - tain What ligh' - tens the plain; What glist - ens and— spark - les O'er— fair— Beth - le - hem. It bright - ens the heav - ens It— gleams through the night, O Je - su, dear Je - su Thy— glo - ry and light, O Je - su, dear— Je - su Thy— glo - ry and light.

2. What thou - sands ob - serve it What mil - lions re - joice To - geth - er all— sing - ing With one— heart and voice. Still lead - ing, re - veal - ing We— plead once a - gain, O Je - su, dear Je - su Bring peace to all men, O Je - su, dear— Je - su Bring peace to all men.

Carols from *Sing Noël,* compiled by Mary A. Sanders and **Ann Roos.**

GOD REST YOU MERRY GENTLEMEN

Traditional

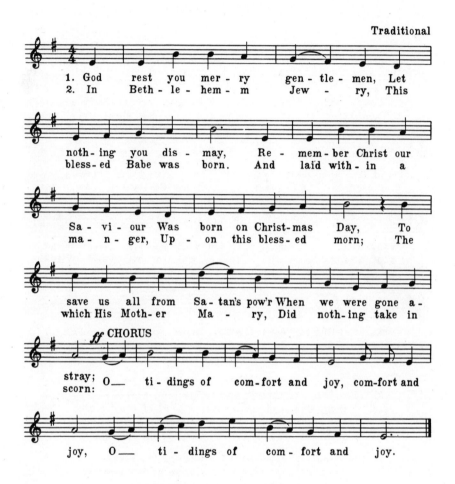

1. God rest you mer - ry gen - tle - men, Let
2. In Beth - le - hem - m Jew - ry, This

noth - ing you dis - may, Re - mem - ber Christ our
bless - ed Babe was born. And laid with - in a

Sa - vi - our Was born on Christ - mas Day, To
ma - n - ger, Up - on this bless - ed morn; The

save us all from Sa - tan's pow'r When we were gone a -
which His Moth - er Ma - ry, Did noth - ing take in

ff CHORUS

stray; O— ti - dings of com - fort and joy, com - fort and
scorn:

joy, O— ti - dings of com - fort and joy.

3. Now to the Lord sing praises,
   All you within this place,
   And with true love and brotherhood
   Each other now embrace;
   This holy tide of Christmas
   All other doth deface.
   Chorus: O tidings, etc.

171

WASSAIL SONG

Gloucestershire

1. Was - sail, was - sail, _ all o - ver the town; Our
2. Then here's to the horse, and to his right eye! _ May

bread it is white and our ale _ it _ is brown. Our
God send our mas - ter a good Christ - mas pie, A

bowl it _ is _ made of the white ma - ple tree: With the
good Christ - mas pie that may we all see! With the

cresc.   *poco rit.*   *mf a tempo*

was - s'ling bowl we'll drink un - to Thee!
was - s'ling bowl we'll drink un - to Thee!

3. Then here's to the ox, and to his long tail!
    Pray God send our master a bowl of strong ale,
A bowl of strong ale that may we all see!
    With the wass'ling bowl we'll drink unto Thee!

4 Come, butler, come fill us a bowl of the best!
    Then we hope that your soul in heaven may rest.
But if you do draw us a bowl of the small,
    May the devil take butler, bowl, and all!

5. Then here's to the maid in the lily white smock,
    Who tripp'd to the door and slipp'd back the lock,
Who tripp'd to the door and pull'd back the pin.
    For to let these jolly wassailers walk in.

6. Wassail, wassail all over the town;
    Our bread it is white and our ale it is brown
Our bowl it is made of the white maple tree!
    With the wass'ling bowl we'll drink to Thee!

BOARS HEAD CAROL

Old English

1. The boar's head in hand bear I, Be-
2. The boar's head as I un-der-stand Is the

decked with bays and rose-ma-ry And I pray you my mas-ters
fair-est dish in all this land which thus be-decked with a

be mer-ry, Quot es-tis-in con-vi-vi-o
gay gar-land Let us ser-vi-re can-ti-co

Ca-put a-pri de-fe-ro Red-dens lau-des Do-mi-no.

Chorus after each verse

3. Our steward hath provided this
   In honour of the King of bliss
   Which on this day to be served is.
   In Reginensi atrio.

THE TWELVE DAYS OF CHRISTMAS

Traditional

1. On the first — day of Christ - mas my true love sent to me A par-tridge in a pear tree.

2. On the sec-ond day of Christ-mas my true love sent to me Two tur-tle doves and a par-tridge in a pear tree.

3. On the third day of Christmas my true love sent to me Three French hens, Two tur-tle doves and a par-tridge in a pear tree.

4. On the fourth — day of Christ - mas my true love sent to me Four call-ing birds, Three French hens, Two tur-tle doves and a par-tridge in a pear tree.

5. On the fifth day of Christ-mas my true love sent to me

Five gold _ rings, Four calling birds, Three French hens,

Two tur-tle doves and a par-tridge in a pear tree.

6. On the sixth day of Christmas my true love sent to me

A   **B**

Six geese a-lay-ing, Five gold _ rings,

Four _ call-ing birds, Three French hens,

Two tur-tle doves and a par-tridge in a pear tree.

7. On the seventh day of Christmas my true love sent to me Seven swans a-swimming.
8. On the eighth day of Christmas my true love sent to me Eight maids a-milking.
9. On the ninth day of Christmas my true love sent to me Nine ladies dancing.
10. On the tenth day of Christmas my true love sent to me Ten Lords a-leaping.
11. On the eleventh day of Christmas my true love sent to me Eleven pipers piping.
12. On the twelfth day of Christmas my true love sent to me Twelve drummers drumming.

A - B   Repeat this measure as often as necessary, the text in reverse order, always ending with "two turtle doves, etc."

175

BRING A TORCH, JEANNETTE, ISABELLA

Allegretto

Old French Carol

1. Bring a torch, ___ Jean-nette, Is-a-bel-la!
2. It is wrong when the Child ___ is sleep-ing,
3. Soft-ly to _____ the lit-tle sta-ble,

Bring a torch, to the cra-dle run!
It is wrong ___ to talk ___ so loud;
Soft-ly for _____ a mo-ment come;

It is Je-sus, good folk of the vil-lage;
Si-lence, all, as you gath-er a-round, ___
Look and see ___ how charm-ing is Je-sus,

Christ is born, and Ma-ry's call-ing; Ah,
Lest ___ your noise should wak-en Je-sus: Hush,
How He is white, His cheeks are ro-sy: Hush,

ah! Beau-ti-ful is the moth-er! Ah,
hush! See ___ how fast He slum-bers: Hush,
hush! See how the Child is sleep-ing: Hush,

ah! Beau-ti-ful is her Son! ___
hush! See ___ how fast He sleeps! ___
hush! See how He smiles in dreams! ___

DECK THE HALLS

Old Welsh Air

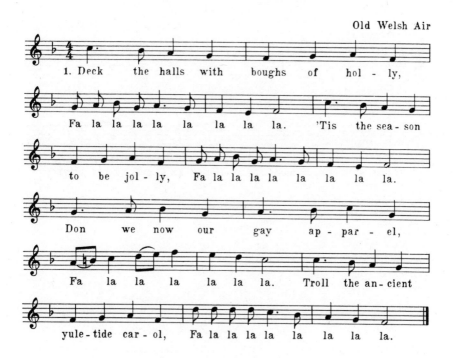

1. Deck the halls with boughs of hol - ly,
Fa la la la la la la la la. 'Tis the sea - son
to be jol - ly, Fa la la la la la la la la.
Don we now our gay ap - par - el,
Fa la la la la la. Troll the an - cient
yule - tide car - ol, Fa la la la la la la la la.

2. See the blazing yule before us,
    Fa la la la la la la la la.
Strike the harp and join the chorus,
    Fa la la la la la la la la.
Follow me in merry measure,
    Fa la la la la la la la la.
While I tell of yule-tide treasure,
    Fa la la la la la la la la.

3. Fast away the old year passes,
    Fa la la la la la la la la.
Hail the new, ye lads and lassies,
    Fa la la la la la la la la.
Sing we joyous all together,
    Fa la la la la la la la la.
Heedless of the wind and weather,
    Fa la la la la la la la la.

177

ONCE, LONG AGO

Brightly

Old Bohemian Christmas Carol

1. Once, long a - go, when the world lay_ a - sleep,
2. Then all_ the_ skies were a - flame with great light,

Out on_ the_ plain shep-herds watch'd o'er their sheep;
Where shin-ing_ hosts of_ God's an - gels stood bright;

HERE WE COME A'WASSAILING

Traditional

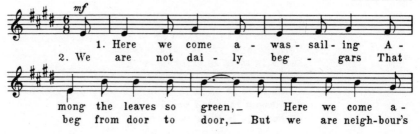

1. Here we come a - was - sail - ing A -
2. We are not dai - ly beg - gars That

mong the leaves so green,_ Here we come a -
beg from door to door,_ But we are neigh-bour's

wan - d'ring, So fair _____ to be seen.
child - ren Whom you have seen be - fore.

CHORUS

Love and joy come to you, And to you, your was-sail
too, And God bless you, and send you A hap - py New
Year, And God send you a hap-py New_ Year.

VERSE

3. Good Master and good Mistress
   As you sit by the fire,
   Pray think of us poor children
   Who are wandering in the mire.
   Love and joy, etc.

4. We have a little purse
   Made of ratching* leather skin;
   We want some of your small change
   To line it well within.
   Love and joy, etc.

5. Bring us out a table,
   And spread it with a cloth;
   Bring us out a mouldy cheese,
   And some of your Christmas loaf.
   Love and joy, etc.

6. God bless the master of this house,
   Likewise the mistress too;
   And all the little children
   That round the table go.
   Love and joy, etc.

*Leather that will stretch.

179